ISSUE 01

WOODSKILLS

The semiannual magazine for the discerning, modern fine woodworking enthusiast

STUDY WOODWORKERS
PROFILES

learn their methods, see their studio spaces. Discover what inspires their work

HOW TO IMPROVE YOUR
STUDIO

an efficiently laid out, clean woodworking studio is conducive to good work

DISCOVER HAND TOOL
TECHNIQUES

grasp new methods of work. Increase your woodworking efficiency

DISCOVER TOOLS TO WORK
WOOD

the why and how of tools to create joinery and smooth surfaces of wood

TABLE OF CONTENTS

WOODSKILLS Magazine
Issue 01

Editor
Norman Pirollo

Art Director
Linda Chenard

Layout
John Pirollo

Copy Editor
Norman Pirollo
Editorial Staff
Volunteers

Publisher
New Art Press

Contributors

Jacques Breau
Alexandra Climent
Philip Morley
Norman Pirollo

newart
P R E S S

Editorial Contributions
norman@woodskills.com

www.woodskills.com
twitter.com/WoodSkills
facebook.com/WoodSkills
Instagram: @woodskillsmag

FROM THE EDITOR

Welcome to the first issue of WOODSKILLS magazine. After careful analysis and research of existing woodworking magazines, we wish to deliver to you a unique and different type of publication. The magazine will only include a small selection of quality, curated advertising. WOODSKILLS magazine will primarily include fine woodworking articles and profiles of established woodworkers and furniture makers. These are woodworkers who excel at what they do and offer an insight into the techniques and work methods they have developed.

Included with each of the profiles are the inspiration and philosophy behind the woodworker and furniture maker. Although machines are often used in the preliminary processing of wood, the vast majority of work in each WOODSKILLS article will be performed using a selection of quality hand tools. We sincerely hope you enjoy the magazine and look forward to producing quality content for your continued woodworking enjoyment.

Norman Pirollo

STUDIO PRACTICES

A general discussion of the optimal furniture studio and woodworking environment. Combining hand tools and workbenches with machines

by Norman Pirollo

An advantage of an established and long woodworking career is the knowledge of what workshop layout works best. In these next few pages, I wish to share this knowledge with you. My former workshop was in a small, cramped basement room with minimal dust collection and little space between workstations. My new, current workshop has addressed these criteria in spades. I find that an unobstructed work environment with minimal clutter is conducive to good woodworking. For the enjoyment of woodworking, clutter and messiness should be avoided. Other criteria include sufficient ambient light delivered through large windows. Ambient, natural light is better on the eyes and allows furniture components to be seen in a natural setting.

In this series of photos, a combination of machines, power tools and hand tools can be seen. Although I profess to working primarily with hand tools, machines provide a quick and efficient method of preparing boards for use in furniture projects. I prefer to call this the grunt work of woodworking. A rigid, practical and solid workbench is overwhelmingly the basis of any hand tool work. Often used in conjunction with a workbench are bench accessories. Bench accessories serve as aids for efficient work holding and processing of work when using hand tools. In a typical hand tool workshop, bench accessories are both necessary and critical in maintaining a demanding pace of work.

Workshop, hand tools and workbench all come together to create an environment conducive to woodworking. A peaceful, serene area in which we can unleash our creativity and develop hand to eye skills.

The photos at the right feature several often used bench accessories. These accessories have evolved over the centuries. The common theme is that they are used to hold work for hand tool operations. Pictured at right is the common woodworking vise. This particular model is all metal with wood faces added on. This vise was installed on the very first woodworking bench I built. Although this vise is very effective, the ideal woodworking vise had dual guide rods spaced further apart with solid hardwood faces attached to a lead screw.

The shooting board shown at right excels at accurately trimming the ends of boards. Shooting boards are typically shop-made, although there are a couple available on the market. The shooting board is considered a precision instrument. When used in conjunction with a hand plane on its side, extremely fine slivers can be trimmed from the end of a board. Attachments also allow mitered cuts to be trimmed. In my furniture studio, I use the shooting board very regularly in my work. So much so that I have two shooting boards, one at each of my large workbenches. The shooting boards are set up for both square and miter trimming through the removable attachments shown.

A selection of workholding bench accessories can be seen at the right. I developed these accessories a number of years ago to overcome the difficulty of holding small to medium wood components while hand planing them. They range from different sized planing stops to bird's mouth stops. The bird's mouth stops are effective at holding small parts on edge. These accessories share the common element of a length of dowel. A short length of dowel is used to attach each of the bench accessories to the workbench surface using preexisting dog holes in the top.

BENCH ACCESSORIES

Workshop, hand tools and workbench all come together to create an environment conducive to woodworking. A peaceful, serene area in which we can unleash our creativity and develop hand to eye skills.

Location of the workbench is an important criteria in efficient workshop workflow. In my previous workshop, there was insufficient space to be able to place my workbench in an ideal setting. It was therefore placed against a wall, this removed access to the opposite side of the workbench. In my current workshop with its increased space, I chose to locate the workbenches away from outside walls. This allows me complete access to all four sides of a workbench. Since I use workholding devices on both long edges of my workbenches, the free space surrounding each workbench has been a boon to my workflow. Space surrounding a workbench is something to consider with your own workbench and work space. Optimally, a workbench should be away from a wall as seen in the photo on the previous page. Directly behind the workbench in the corner is a router station.

Photos on the previous page also show how machines can be combined with workbenches in a workshop. Ideally, machines should be in their own room to contain dust generated and to keep the area isolated from the hand tool area. In my own workshop, there is insufficient space to afford this luxury. The next best option is to combine machine stations and hand tool benches in the same space. The inclusion of effective dust collection becomes critical for this option to work. My former shop was a dusty mess and no manner of dust control could contain the dust. At the time, I hardly worked with hand tools. A few years later I developed an exclusive hand tool style of woodworking. This change dramatically reduced the dust generated in my work. Today, I work primarily with hand tools.

Workshop, hand tools and workbench all come together to create an environment conducive to woodworking. A peaceful, serene area in which we can unleash our creativity and develop hand to eye skills.

The photo series at left features often used bench accessories. These accessories are designed for individual applications. At the left, a sliding board jack holds the end of a board up on edge for jointing the edge. Various dog holes have been bored into the board jack to hold boards of different widths. The sliding board jack has evolved over the centuries to this more modern version. These bench accessories are designed to be adaptable to any workbench. Their simplicity is their strong point. They can be easily created by a woodworker and excel as aids to the woodworker in their furniture making. They can be made using commonly available wood and hardware.

The dovetail jig shown at the left excels at aligning the tail and pin boards for accurate marking. An example of this can be seen in the photo. The cleats hold the workpieces tightly against both the vertical and horizontal surfaces. This jig or accessory can easily be created in a few hours. When creating dovetail joints, an accurate transfer of markings from one board to the other is critical. Simply holding the boards together is not sufficient. Bench accessories such as this excel in aiding a woodworker in creating precise joinery.

The edge dogs at left are designed to hold boards on edge for jointing. This clever design incorporates dowels that fit into a workbench top. Not all workbenches have aprons or skirts at the side to fasten bench dogs or clamps to. Edge dogs solve this dilemma by attaching to the workbench top instead. This is an example of how versatile bench accessories can be at aiding your woodworking with common operations performed on a bench. The edge dogs are not difficult to create and are made using leftover wood from furniture builds.

BENCH ACCESSORIES

Workshop, hand tools and workbench all come together to create an environment conducive to woodworking. A peaceful, serene area in which we can unleash our creativity and develop hand to eye skills.

The reference to studio practices involves not only the use of bench accessories but the work methods oriented around your workspace. The work methodology that furniture makers and woodworkers become accustomed to revolves around the type of woodworking they perform in their respective workshops. When asked for advice around setting up a workshop, I often mention to a woodworker or prospective furniture maker to work with an initial layout for a while. A work flow will slowly evolve, much like the work triangle in a kitchen. So it does depend heavily on what machines and workbenches you use to perform your tasks. Case in point, my own furniture studio continues to evolve with the addition of wall mounted cabinets to store tools. As well, other enhancements to improve work flow have been implemented over the years.

Shown above is a fairly recent bench accessory created to solve a dilemma I was facing. The dilemma of how to hold long wide boards on my primary workbenches in order to joint their long edges. Since both my primary workbenches were not designed with aprons, a method to clamp or hold boards at their far end is not available. This small addition to the underside of the workbench solves the dilemma. It is designed to be portable between my two workbenches as well as being unobtrusive. Today, I simply leave it attached to the workbench top as seen. This provides an excellent example of the importance of developing your own bench accessories specific to your furniture making or woodworking. In other words, some bench accessories are general in nature, whereas others are specific to a particular operation.

Workshop, hand tools and workbench all come together to create an environment conducive to woodworking. A peaceful, serene area in which we can unleash our creativity and develop hand to eye skills.

Common to several of the bench accessories in this article is the dowel, also recognized as a bench dog. The lowly bench dog has been in use throughout past centuries and evolved from a workbench peg used during the Roman era. The premise is to insert a dowel or bench dog into the workbench top where it typically serves as a stop. As seen in the photo below, one side of the dowel has a flat face to align better with the square end of a board. Bench dogs are versatile in that they can quickly be inserted or removed from a bench top.

As well, bench dogs can be easily raised or lowered. Although round bench dogs are primarily used individually, they are often used in their most basic dowel form to attach bench accessories to a workbench surface. Since dog holes have already been bored in a workbench top, why not simply use dowels inserted into these holes to hold accessories. A few accessories were shown earlier and several more can be seen in the lower right hand photo. In the photo below right, a series of attachments to a planing board can be seen.

As well, standalone bench accessories which insert directly into the workbench top are seen. These planing stops, bird's mouth stops, and lateral guides were developed a number of years ago in my workshop. They work as a system with attachments that plug into a planing board using a series of dowels with predetermined hole spacing. The planing board itself then plugs into the workbench surface using large diameter dowels.

When the planing board and attachments are used together, this system excels as a simple and versatile method of holding boards from moving forward or sideways while hand planing their faces or edges. The versatility of dowels and bench dogs can be appreciated through these accessories. In my own studio practice, I strive to find the simplest and most reliable method to hold work for bench operations. I find the simplest methods get used repeatedly since there is so little set up time involved. This can be viewed this as a minimalist approach to work holding.

BENCH ACCESSORIES

Workshop, hand tools and workbench all come together to create an environment conducive to woodworking. A peaceful, serene area in which we can unleash our creativity and develop hand to eye skills.

BENCH TECHNIQUES

Discussion on the process of developing your own bench techniques and hand tool processes. How to improve on the workflow in your workshop.

by Norman Pirollo

Bench accessories have been discussed in the last few pages. In this article, I would like to discuss techniques of working wood at a workbench. Once you have decided on an optimal placement of your workbench, the next logical step is to develop an efficient workflow around the bench. This involves several factors, one of which is whether you are left or right-handed. I mention this since I am left-handed and need to orient myself differently than a right-handed woodworker. Since most bench operations involve pushing a hand plane, the direction of hand plane travel is a large factor in where vises are located. The type of vise and placement of vises on a workbench does also depend on the scale of your work. Conventional wisdom states that a face vise is necessary for a workbench. The face vise provides clamping of boards or wood components along their face. A face vise can be seen in the photo below.

The next most common bench vise is the tail vise. A tail vise is used primarily to fasten one end of a board to a workbench surface. The other end is typically placed against a bench dog. When used in conjunction with each other, the tail vise and bench dog excel at holding a workpiece for hand planing operations. The caveat is that this workholding is ideally suited to boards oriented with their faces on the workbench surface. Although it can work for boards on edge, the boards need to be narrow. For wider boards, an alternative system needs to be in place. The tail vise will need to somehow extend to the side of the workbench. This allows long, wide boards to be placed against the side of a workbench, increasing the versatility of the workbench. Below is a photo of an edge dog. The edge dog successfully clamps one end of a board along the side of the workbench.

DEVELOP BENCH TECHNIQUES
RADICALLY IMPROVE YOUR WOODWORKING AND BRING IT TO THE NEXT LEVEL

Discussion on the process of developing your own bench techniques and hand tool processes. How to best utilize your workbench to create a more efficient environment in which to perform woodworking

Your direction of movement precludes the orientation of your bench vise. Do you tend to work left to right or right to left. In my own work, I can work in either direction since the workbench is located away from a wall. This criteria is critical to the enjoyment of your woodworking. I recall experimenting with several workbench layouts before my latest setup. If you have been struggling with workholding and clamping work to your workbench, experiment with alternative vise orientations. Ensure that the vises and clamping setups you utilize are strong and stable. If the configuration doesn't work for you, change it!

Other bench techniques involve use of the previously mentioned bench accessories. As an example, I use the dovetail jig to transfer marks from tail to pin boards. The dovetail jig is simply placed against the long edge of a workbench, and then removed once the work has been completed. Bench hooks are another example. These are also placed along a workbench edge and are used to saw small components to size. The shooting board is placed against the workbench edge through use of a cleat. Shooting boards are used to accurately trim the ends of boards using a slicing action, and leave a fine surface.

Over time, you will develop a strategy of how best to work wood components on your workbench. There are several workbench layouts available. They range from Roubo, Nicholson to European and North American styled workbenches. Each bench style addresses a specific need. The style of workbench used in my studio is a commercial unit modeled after a Scandinavian design. The Roubo and Nicholson style of workbenches were used in earlier centuries prior to modern advancements.

BENCH TECHNIQUES OF PARING WITH A CHISEL AND CREATING A CHAMFER

BENCH TECHNIQUES OF
CLAMPING WORK AND
HAND PLANING
Using tail vise to clamp
board for flattening

Once your ideal and most effective workholding has been established, you can begin to work on standard bench techniques. The workbench is used in most common hand plane operations. The typical sequence would be to flatten a board using longer planes, thickness the board, and finally dimension the board in both width and length. In the photo above, the board has just been flattened and is being tested for flatness along its length. The next logical step would be to determine its flatness across its width and then diagonally, for good measure. If working exclusively with hand tools, these steps will be repeated for every board you use in your furniture or woodworking project.

It can be seen how important a strong and rigid workbench becomes part of the process of creating accurate furniture components. Workbenches are built to be massive in both size and weight. Over centuries the heft of a typical workbench has been reduced due to better fastening and joinery. Today the workbench, although still heavy with large components, is considerably lighter than its earlier counterparts. The workbenches in my furniture studio are commercially available and designed to be knock-down or easily disassembled.

It is generally recommended to build your own workbench as it is considered a skill-building rite of passage. Having already built a few workbenches early in my woodworking progression, I opted instead to purchase two well-designed workbenches. The earlier workbenches tended to err on the heavy, stout side and I soon realized that moving them would be a challenge. More recently, I decided on a compromise of strong yet lighter workbenches. An advantage of the two commercially available workbenches in my furniture studio is standardization. My bench accessories and jigs are portable between the workbenches.

WORKING WITH HAND PLANES, CHISELS AND SCRAPERS

by Norman Pirollo

Discussion on the process of developing your own bench techniques and hand tool processes. How to best utilize your workbench to create a more efficient environment in which to perform woodworking

Hand planes, chisels and scrapers are the mainstays of any hand tool woodworking shop. Other hand tools are equally important, primarily measuring, marking and other shaping tools such as spokeshaves. The three tools mentioned first are most often used to dress and shape wood. As an argument to the importance of hand planes, several different types of hand planes are available, each dedicated to a particular application.

Hand planes are available to prepare rough wood, to joint the edges of wood, to dimension wood, and for the final smoothing of wood. The most obvious difference in each of these hand planes is their length. The length determines their application. Longer planes are best suited to flattening wood surfaces and for jointing the edges of wood. Mid-length planes are more versatile and are used for jointing and preparing or smoothing wood surfaces. The smoothing plane is well suited to final smoothing of wood surfaces.

A small block plane used to shape small components at left. A set of bevel-edge chisels to create dovetails at right.

The chisel is arguably the most often used hand tool along with the hand plane. In my own studio, I have three sets of bevel-edge chisels at my disposal along with a set of mortise chisels for hogging out larger bits of wood. Chisels are used to shape parts, to create chamfers, to clean dovetail sockets and to create mortises. These are a small sampling of tasks where chisels excel. When equipping a hand tool workshop, a good set of chisels is necessary.

Higher quality chisels maintain their sharp edge longer and are more resistant to chipping of metal at their edge. A regular honing regimen needs to be developed and maintained to keep chisels and hand plane irons continually sharp. A quality set of chisels contributes heavily to the development of effective bench techniques. Sharp tools are your friend in the workshop.

SCRAPER BLADE ON
WOOD SURFACE

scraping action slices
wood fibers instead of
abrading them

 The scraper, although simple and plain in appearance, is arguably one of the most effective hand tools in a workshop. The scraper may appear as a rectangular piece of flexible metal, but in reality it outperforms another common form of smoothing a wood surface. Scrapers replace sanding in a hand tool workshop. The business end of a scraper blade incorporates a cleverly created burr which serves to mimic a hand plane. When using a scraper to finish a wood surface, there is dramatically less incidence of tearout. Tearout can be devastating, especially in figured woods. Figured woods are very prone to tearout, and this is where the scraper blade excels.

The versatility of scraper blades is also demonstrated by the virtue that they can be pushed forward or pulled back along a wood surface. It is critical to maintain a slight curve in the spring metal to create the slicing action. This action slices or shears a layer of wood fibers with every pass. Sandpaper instead abrades the fibers resulting in a dull finish. Scraped surfaces maintain a depth and clarity when a finish is applied due to the clean, slicing action.

One of the distinct advantages of using hand tools in a workshop or furniture studio is the relative dust free environment created. Hand planes, chisels and scrapers only produce shavings. The advantages to this are numerous, including the diminished incidence of allergic reactions to airborne wood dust. Airborne wood dust can create an allergic reaction in the lungs and nasal passages. Through the action of hand tools, airborne dust is instead virtually eliminated. In my own studio, although I pre-process wood using machines, an effective dust collection system contains most of the dust created. The other advantage to using hand tools is a quiet and noise free work environment. Without the drone of machines, a peaceful and quiet workshop environment is considerably more enjoyable and conducive to woodworking.

THE SHOOTING BOARD
BRING PERFECTION AND ACCURACY TO YOUR WORK

by Norman Pirollo

Discussion on the benefits and accuracy a shooting board can bring to your workshop practices. Shooting board techniques are described as well as the use of shooting board attachments for trimming of mitered components.

As we strive towards getting the perfectly square joint, it is often difficult to achieve with the tools and machinery we have at our disposal. One or a few bad adjustments can multiply and instead provide us with a close to but not perfectly square joint or miter. The time-proven method to ensure that corners and miters on smaller boards are square is to use a shooting board. The shooting board was developed over a century ago to address this very issue.

The shooting board is especially suited to thinner work which cannot be easily hand planed due to the narrow bearing surface. A good example of narrower stock are the components of a small drawer for a jewelry box or small cabinet. Another example is the face frame of a small cabinet with thin, narrow rails and stiles. A shooting board can be created to be as simple as possible or assembled with a few extra features which make it a greater pleasure to use.

In the photos below of a shop-made shooting board, there are two attached levels of baltic birch plywood. The top level (baseboard) is narrower than the bottom. This creates a lower runway at the right which enables the side of a hand plane to have a surface to glide on. This surface guides the hand plane from the front to the back of the shooting board as in the photo below right. A fence which is installed onto the baseboard of the shooting board is also seen.

As shown below, there is a hint of a gap between the fence and upper edge of the runway and the sole of the hand plane. This gap is typically the width of a shaving the hand plane will take, between 1-3,000 / inch. Also seen is the leading edge of the blade shaving the mitered cherry board while just sliding by the fence.

LEFT, TAPED AREA KEEPS PLANE SOLE FROM PLANING RUNWAY. BELOW, DETAIL WHERE PLANE SOLE MEETS FENCE

SHOOTING BOARD
WITH FACE MITER
ATTACHMENT

used to trim face-
mitered and edge-
mitered ends of
boards

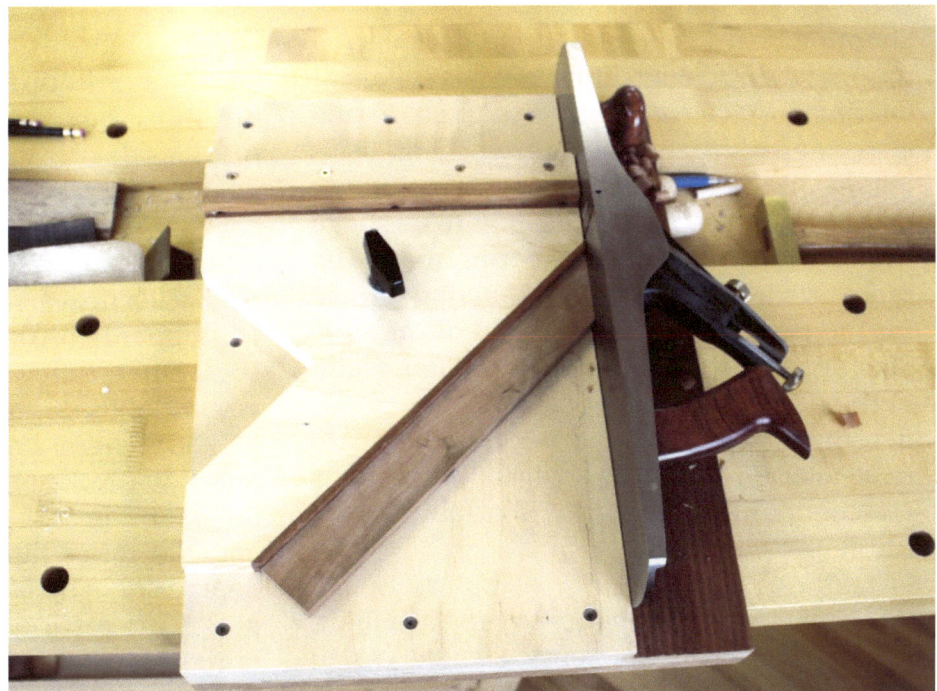

The fence is composed of a fixed, lighter component with a dark hardwood face screwed horizontally to the fixed component. This set up allows for adjustment of the dark hardwood face. This enables the fence to be perfectly perpendicular to the edge of the shooting board runway, without the need to remove the fixed portion. The dark area at the junction of the lower runway and edge of the upper level (baseboard) serves as a guide for the hand plane sole. You can avoid a runway and simply use your bench top as a surface to glide the hand plane along. In this case, ensure that the bench top is flat. The runway provides a guarantee that the hand plane side or wing will glide along a perfectly flat surface. The position of the fence should be between the end and middle of the shooting board. This provides a continuous motion of the hand plane well past the board being squared. A cleat is also visible in the photo above. The cleat hooks the shooting board onto the edge of your bench, effectively using the bench to clamp the shooting board.

A number of different hand planes can be used for this operation. Ideally a larger, heavier plane is best suited due to its increased mass and stability. Once momentum is established, the actual shooting process requires little effort. The depth adjustment of the blade is minimally set at first with very small increments dialed in. Key is to strive for very thin shavings off the end of the board. It will be harder to push the plane with thicker shavings and the hand plane will likely bind. The board is held against both the fence and the sole of the hand plane. Very light pressure is necessary as the hand plane itself pushes the board against the fence. The hand plane requires only minimal pressure sideways. Rocking of the hand plane is to be avoided. The only real pressure is the forward motion of the hand plane along the runway. It should be mentioned that hand planes with larger wings or side surfaces fare better on shooting boards. Larger wings keep the plane stable and make it easier to keep square on the runway.

Shooting board components are optimally in the 3/4 in. thick range. This provides sufficient bearing surface for the sole to glide on and also keeps the plane from rocking. It is important to keep from rocking the plane as this causes unnecessary shavings to be sliced from the fence area of the shooting board. The fence provides both a stop and bearing surface for the workpiece to be squared or mitered. The fence must be completely perpendicular to the path of the hand plane sole, since this determines how square the end of the board is in relation to its long edge. The fence is attached with screws and adjustable in the future for wear.

It is necessary for the fence to remain square to the runway as the fence also serves to eliminate tearout of the board being trimmed. Tearout is the shearing of fibers at the back corner edge of a board. In the photo at left the end of a small cherry board is measured for square. The long edge of the board serves as a reference surface for the engineer's square. Ensure you create a straight edge on the board being squared prior to shooting the end of the board. This edge will be the reference surface used against the fence of the shooting board. With both edges of the board straight and parallel to each other, the board can be flipped and either long edge used as a reference surface. This provides an accurately squared end of the board.

MITER ATTACHMENT OF SHOOTING BOARD TESTING SQUARE ENDS OF A BOARD, BOTH PERPENDICULAR AND AT 45 DEGREES

Shown below is the shooting board miter attachment in operation. The end of a small box side is being planed for a 45-degree miter. All four sides of the box will be planed the same way ensuring the miter joints fit correctly. Light shavings are taken off the end with particular attention in keeping the board firmly against the backer board. This will ensure that the edge of the board with the miter being tuned remains square to the side of the board. Shown below is the front view of the shooting board miter jig and a cherry board bring trued or tuning a miter on. Notice the barely noticeable gap between the sole of the wooden hand plane and the miter jig ramp. Instead, the cherry board is right up against the blade of the hand plane. The gap is only slightly greater than the original gap between the plane sole and the shooting board runway side. The board being mitered needs to be of uniform thickness across its width for the mitered surface to be accurate.

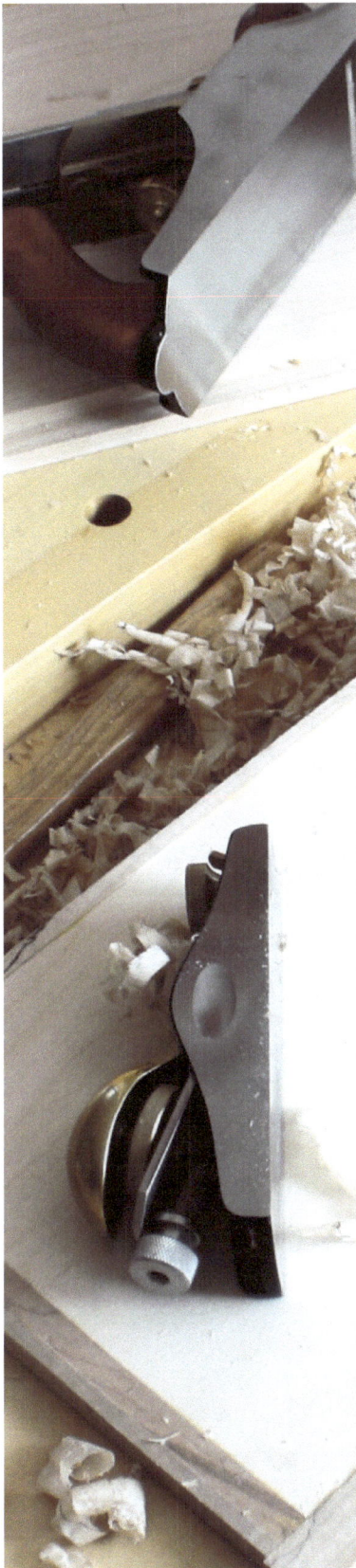

Making your own shooting board can be considered a rite of passage in the hand tool philosophy of woodworking. A shooting board can either be made quickly or with more time, an enhanced version created with more features. The quick and dirty version is simply a board with a squared fence and a cleat at the bottom to hold it against a workbench top. A more elaborate version will have an adjustable fence and be able to accept attachments such as those discussed in this article. The shooting board I decided on has an adjustable fence, a replaceable fence, and accepts attachments. It is more of a long term design rather than a quick version. Key to a shooting board is the accuracy between the fence and the runway. It is necessary to have this perfectly at 90 degrees since every board end you shoot will be a consequence of this measurement.

A few years ago, I contributed an article to an established woodworking magazine. The subject was bench jigs and the shooting board design shown on these pages was included in the article. I made a left and right-hand version of the shooting board for the article. Since I am left-handed and the vast majority of woodworkers are right-handed, this made perfect sense. Today I use both of the shooting boards in my furniture studio. One shooting board is set up for square ends whereas the second shooting board is set for miters.

The shooting board fits into my workflow as a final step in the dimensioning or trimming of the ends of boards. If the board is not very wide and small in dimension, I typically trim a board close to final size on the bandsaw. This leaves a not smooth but ragged edge. The length of board or workpiece is then slightly longer than its final size. The shooting board is then used for final dimensioning and to create a very smooth, square end. For wider and longer boards, I tend to use a precision fence system on a table saw. This will be the subject of a future article in this magazine.

SHOOTING BOARD WITH EDGE MITER ATTACHMENT

NORMAN PIROLLO
AN ARTISTIC TOUCH TO FURNITURE DESIGN

Discussion on how to incorporate elements of art and figured woods into a furniture design. How to visualize a furniture design through an artistic eye. The technique of enhancing a furniture design through the addition of color.

A few years ago, the use of figured woods introduced a new aesthetic into my work and furniture designs. No longer did furniture need to be uniform in grain and consistent in appearance. Figured woods could enhance the appeal of my furniture. The focal point could shift to the figured wood as well as to the overall design. Figured woods can be interpreted as nature's own abstract wood art. Furniture incorporating figured wood is purely functional but features an element of art. Every board of figured wood exhibits slightly different characteristics from another board of the same species. Continuity between slices is achieved through a method of resawing slices to form a flitch and then slip-matching them together. There is considerably less clash in wood graphics when using this approach. Book-matching is a method of joining figured wood veneer slices. Veneer slices are joined at their common edge so the pattern becomes a mirror image on both sides of the veneer sheet.

With several methods to choose from of combining wood slices into a veneer sheet, there are several possibilities available when using figured wood veneers in a furniture piece. It was in this period of furniture making that I began to incorporate highly figured veneers into several of my display cabinet designs. Creating veneer slices allowed me to extract greater yields from highly figured boards. Sawing a board into several thin slices was an efficient use of wood from the board. Veneered surfaces are primarily decorative, and it made little sense to use the complete thickness of a board for door or side panels. I was drawn to figured wood veneers through early experiments with veneering. Each highly figured board provided an abstract pattern of grain where slicing the board would reveal even more interesting patterns. In furniture making, these patterns are commonly referred to as wood graphics. A collection of figured woods is always maintained in my wood storage. The figured woods are in the form of sliced veneers or boards. The boards are then sliced into shop-sawn veneers and applied to a core or substrate.

Attaching a sheet of veneer to a substrate is the most cost effective and efficient use of highly figured woods. Veneered panels using shop-sawn veneers are often indistinguishable from solid board variants of the same figured woods. Highly figured wood can be very expensive although this depends on the amount and quality of the figure. The species of wood is also a criterion in determining the price of figured wood. Figured woods are not limited to domestic wood species. Often, figure is found in exotic wood species. When out shopping for wood, I often peruse the figured wood section of a wood retailer to seek out an unusually figured board. I do not hesitate to purchase it. In all likelihood, it will otherwise be sold to another buyer.

Over time, I began to incorporate figured woods into my furniture pieces. It is critical to properly use figured woods in a furniture design. Although I have created display cabinet designs with a large proportion of figured woods, it is wise to limit the use of figured woods when introducing figured woods into your own furniture designs. The use of figured woods was ramped up in certain furniture pieces only after I became familiar with the characteristics of veneered panels. A best practice is to limit the use of veneered figured wood panels to door panels for a cabinet, either within a frame and panel assembly, or as the complete panel of a door. Figured domestic and exotic woods are ideal goods to purchase and hang on to as they have no expiry date and will never be obsolete!

CREATION OF A WOOD SCULPTURE USING FIGURED WOODS

The centuries old French Polishing process used to reveal the depth and clarity of this wood sculpture.

It is also highly advised to only use a single species of figured wood throughout. Otherwise, a distracting, visual clash will occur. Judicious use of figured woods in a furniture piece is recommended as a best practice. Too much of a good thing can destroy the intended aesthetic. The application of figured woods created a new direction in my work. I would constantly be on the lookout for highly figured boards at wood retailers. These are woods that could be resawn into thin veneers. The dimensional stability of veneered panels and more specifically, highly figured ones, became very appealing. Although the process of creating thin veneers from thick boards can be slow and tedious; acquiring several slices of veneers from a single board is extremely cost-effective.

Often, the board is very unique in its characteristics where another board would be markedly different in characteristics. Therefore, acquiring a maximum number of veneer slices from a board is critical in avoiding discontinuity of wood graphics. The sequential veneer slices sawn from a board are considered a flitch of veneers. The flitch is taped together where multiple slices are available to a buyer. This ensures that the grain pattern or figure is matching, an important criterion in furniture making. Having resawn a considerable amount of boards into veneers, I calculate the number of slices necessary and seek boards to acquire the slices from.

NORMAN PIROLLO
WHERE ART + DESIGN MEET

Discussion on how to incorporate elements of art and figured woods into a furniture design. How to visualize a furniture design through an artistic eye. The technique of enhancing a furniture design through the addition of color.

While perusing some maple boards at a big box store, I noticed one board which stood out as being highly figured. The maple board had a rich curl figure. The board was purchased at the same price as other boards of the same wood species and has since been used as veneers in the door panels of my furniture. Commercial lumber mills are often not set up to extract boards with unusual figure. It would be cost prohibitive for the mill to set up a process to isolate both these logs and resulting boards. They are therefore processed as other logs and boards are. Clients seeking processed boards typically purchase wood for the species characteristics and are not seeking highly figured variants of boards. I happened to be in the right place at the right time! Another variant in wood surfaces are the alternating dark and light areas resulting from different wood densities. This characteristic causes stain or finish to be absorbed differently in each area of the surface of a board exhibiting different wood densities.

The result is normally considered blotchy wood, but when viewed through an artistic eye the blotchiness yields a different result. Wood with this blotchy characteristic, when infused with transparent dye, exhibits an interesting and exciting color pattern. Color gradients of the dye applied to the wood surface create a random or abstract wood surface. Highly figured woods are also prized by musical instrument makers. Figured woods are used in the fronts and backs of certain instruments. The more pronounced the figure, the higher the desirability of the board. However, highly figured logs are most often sliced into very thin commercial veneers. Availability of highly figured woods is often sporadic. Retailers or distributors for this type of wood are few and far between.

Retailers that specialize in unusually figured woods can usually be found in and around major urban centers. With the advent of online retail, it is easier to purchase figured woods or veneers today. Most wood retailers specializing in exotic and figured woods process online orders and conveniently ship wood and veneers across the country. In the past, I have traveled to other cities to purchase figured woods. Today, although a variety of figured woods can be purchased locally, I do not hesitate to order online when necessary. While assembling a book-matched selection of veneer slices to create a mirror effect, I became curious to how the veneers would look on a wall. By hanging a veneered panel on a wall, I could easily determine if the idea had aesthetic appeal.

Could a panel of exciting, figured wood become a form of art? My next step was to temporarily create and hang a veneered panel. The panel was prepared with several coats of clear shellac to bring out the depth, clarity and figure of the wood. I convinced myself that if the aesthetic of the panel was not captivating when hung on a wall, the shellac could always be removed, and the panel reused as a component of a furniture piece. Once hung on a wall and viewed in indirect lighting, I was pleasantly surprised at how the figure of the wood came through. A decision was made to further explore the idea. However since the panel was thin, it would be subject to extreme changes in moisture levels.

PROCESS OF CREATING WOOD ART USING HIGHLY FIGURED WOODS

Scale model or maquette of a large wall-mounted wood art installation

High humidity could cause the panel to distort or warp. The panel would therefore, need to be rigidly attached to a box–like structure. The rigid box would provide depth to the panel and keep it from warping in high humidity conditions. This was the woodworker in me developing a solution to a possible problem. Deciding to use this particular panel as a sacrificial panel, a temporary box was created with the thickness of a conventionally framed piece of art. The figured veneer panel was then attached to this box structure and more thin coats of shellac applied to the completed assembly, specifically the showy parts. Once again, the boxed panel was hung on the wall.

The result was more exciting than before since the wood selected for the surrounding box was darker, providing a contrasting frame for the veneered panel. The idea began to have merit. Next, two more boxed panels would be designed and created with more interesting veneers or possibly a combination of veneers. I also began to design the next version of wood art panel using a combination of veneers, some darker, some lighter. This would allow me to create a secondary pattern or graphic on the panel. An example would be a serpentine line where the two veneers slices meet. Using this technique, organic patterns, linear patterns, and geometric patterns could be created on a panel. To be continued in a future article...

Photo by Jacques Breau

JACQUES BREAU
WHEN WOOD MEETS MAKER

by Norman Pirollo

A conversation with a woodworker and furniture maker who applies traditional methods to the creation of modern, Scandinavian influenced furniture designs. His fascinating journey and inspiration are discussed.

The very first thing noticed about Jacques Breau's work is the attention to detail. A close second to this are the clean, modern designs that do not exude ornamentation. Jacques has studied with the best and is a disciple of the Krenov philosophy of woodworking where the wood itself dictates a large part of a design. Ostentatious elements are nowhere to be found in his furniture, just a svelte and modern aesthetic. When first introduced to Jacques, I was immediately drawn to his laid back and peaceful attitude. After seeing his work, I could envision this woodworker quietly slaving away in a serene shop using mostly hand tools. It goes without saying that a huge dose of patience is required to develop the fine craftsmanship in Jacques' handcrafted work.

One has only to lay eyes on his furniture designs to immediately notice the years of skill and talent that he has so obviously acquired. Aside from being a furniture maker and designer, Jacques teaches and guides students along at the Inside Passage School of Fine Woodworking. In conversation with Jacques, he is proud of his lineage and a history of woodworking in his family. Through an upbringing of self-sufficiency, Jacques has learned to cope with the various curve balls thrown at him in the pursuit of a higher level of woodworking. The following questions were put to Jacques to shed more light on this up and coming craftsman and furniture maker. We look forward to seeing more of Jacques' unique and exciting furniture designs.

WS: How and when did you decide to become a woodworker?

JB: I officially took the plunge in 2003. Immediately following the last exam of my undergraduate degree, I hopped into a car with some friends and drove west to attend the Silva Bay Shipyard School. I had a friend there, and we took the Ship's Cabinetry course together. But before I got into that car, I had read a Cabinet Maker's Notebook by James Krenov, Thomas Moser's "How to Build Shaker Furniture", and a decade's worth of Fine Woodworking magazines and was already on my way, in a sense. My dad had a shop at home, and I had tried making some things with varying degrees of success, and I suppose I liked doing that more then anything else I had tried.

WS: Growing up, who and what inspired you to follow a path in woodworking?

JB: I grew up in the country with pretty talented parents. We took care of a lot of things 'in house', gardening, construction projects, sewing, quilting, canning, furnishings... and I was always interested in helping out in the shop. All that to say, that growing up we always made things. Woodworking also runs in my fathers family. His grandfather was a carpenter, and most of my uncles are woodworkers too. I like to say that I got the medium from my father, and my approach from my mother. She is meticulous, precise, patient, and pretty darn good with a sewing machine.

WS: You attended the Inside Passage School, tell us about that experience?

JB: My time as a student at IP was pretty fun. I must have spent a good 60 hours a week down at the school on a regular week and more when show time was approaching. Being that immersed in craft at a high level was like being catapulted a decade ahead in terms of experience. Not to mention the lumber. So much beautiful wood.

During my time there, we were fortunate to have weekly phone lectures from Krenov himself. We would send him questions a few days ahead of time, and he would talk for about an hour. We would all huddle around the speaker phone. It was pretty cool to listen to him speak on all manner of topic. My wife and I got to meet him at his home in Fort Bragg the summer after I did the program. That was pretty neat. He had some of his work in his house (A Playful Thing, the maple off cut cabinet, and some tables) that we got to see.

I was fortunate enough to be able to go back to IP in the years after I studied there to help out as the end of the year show was approaching. I was the evening guy (Robert, the main teacher, was the morning guy), and regularly stayed until the wee hours of the morning helping with glue ups, answering questions, and generally keeping people moving forward with their projects. I think I did that for 4 or 5 years. I learnt a ton doing that. Helping out with a dozen or so projects exposed me to so many different techniques and tricks that I wouldn't have seen in my shop by myself.

WS: You are a furniture designer, maker. What kinds of furniture do you design, make and in what styles?

JB: I make a variety of things for my clients, from painted bathroom vanities to fine wall units. Sometimes the clients taste dictates the style, but if left to my own devises, I tend to design within the Danish modern vocabulary. I tend to like simple, soft, and well proportioned furniture with wood that works to enhance the design without taking over. My speculative work has been veering toward parquetry lately, and mostly seems to be wall hung. For reasons unbeknownst to me, I really like wall hung cabinets. Maybe it's their simplicity, or maybe it's because they lend themselves well to small work spaces.

Photo by Ingeborg Suzanne Hardman

SHOWCASE #2, 2009, ENGLISH BROWN OAK, EASTERN MAPLE, WESTERN MAPLE
11.75" H x 23.75" W x 8.25" D
Jacques Breau Ottawa, Ontario Canada

WS: How would you describe your current work and what inspires it?

JB: Lately I seem to be building mitered case pieces with a heavy Danish modern bent. Mostly commissions, the work is molded to the clients needs and desires. The furniture that I build in my head is more inspired by shapes and tones then anything else. I've been thinking about triangles a lot lately, in the form of mountains and icebergs, and hope to have some time to make a few smallish wall cabinets that explore those shapes.

When I build furniture, I always seem to be running out of material. This forces me to explore thinness and lightness in my work. Furniture parts don't need to be big to do there job, and sometimes light, flexible parts do a better job while maximizing space and materials. Lightness and frugality inspire my work.

WS: Do you have a favorite piece? If so, which one and why?

JB: I've always had a soft spot for Krenov's Yaca and Mahogany cabinet. It may be because of the more modern look, the five sided leg, the inset pulls, or the unattainable wood it's made out of, but it's my favourite cabinet.

WS: Which woods do prefer working with and why?

JB: I prefer stable woods. But all kidding aside, I have a weakness for big planks. I find that the typically available lumber lacks character and charm, mostly because it's all flat sawn. That's not to say that I want all my lumber straight grained, but a little bit of rift sawn never hurt, not to mention being able to match colour and tone across a piece. As far as species are concerned, I don't really have a preference, but I have been hoarding some planks that I can't wait to work with. I have a piece of Yellow Cedar full of bark inclusions, some English Brown Oak, some Pear, some nice Walnut, some big Hard Maple flitches... and I'm just waiting for the time to make something with them. I have ideas for most of the pieces of wood that I've been moving around for the past ten years or so.

WS: Are there any mediums that you haven't worked with yet but hope to in the future?

JB: I've often wanted to use more metal to create texture in my work. I work with metal to make my own hardware, but have never used it to adorn any surface, or as a structural part of a piece. I'm not talking an I beam trestle table base, but more of a material for some type of marquetry or surface texture. I've also been wanting to do more pieces that have glassed in portions. I've had some design ideas in my head for a long time for some more showcase cabinets.

WS: To date, what has been the most rewarding experience involving your furniture and being a woodworker?

JB: Selling pieces to perfect strangers is always a high point. I sold a small box last year to a collector in Buffalo that was made with maple from my grandfather's family farm. I also sold a coffee table to a lady in Amsterdam. Both of these pieces were sold through the Oden Gallery. It's pretty rewarding to know that people connect to the work itself without much else to go on. Next to this, is using my great grandfather's tools. I have a nice cross cut saw of his and my father has a few of his hand planes that I get to borrow sometimes (#4 and #8). It's pretty neat to use a tool the he made his living with.

WS: What advice would you give someone aspiring to become a woodworker or furniture designer?

JB: Work hard, learn to live lean, sketch a lot, build a lot, maybe take a class, marry rich.

Photo by Jacques Breau

WS: What are you currently working on that you would like to mention?

JB: I'm currently working on a cherry sideboard for some lovely people in the Gatineau hills. It's been a pretty fun commission with just the dimensions as a starting point. I've had pretty free reign to fill in the blanks after that.

WS: Are there any upcoming projects and/or events that you would like to mention?

JB: I'm presenting at the Kingston Wood Artisans Symposium in April. I'll be doing a demo on a joint that's in the "Soul of a Tree" by Nakashima, the all end grain corner joint. After that, it's mostly dad duty for me while my wife finishes her Phd thesis. I might get to build something from my wood hoard next year if everything works out.

End Grain Woodworks

Photo by Jacques Breau

DARK HORSE, 2014 WENGE, SPRUCE
24.5" H x 16"W x 8" D
Jacques Breau Ottawa, Ontario Canada

GALLERY
JACQUES BREAU

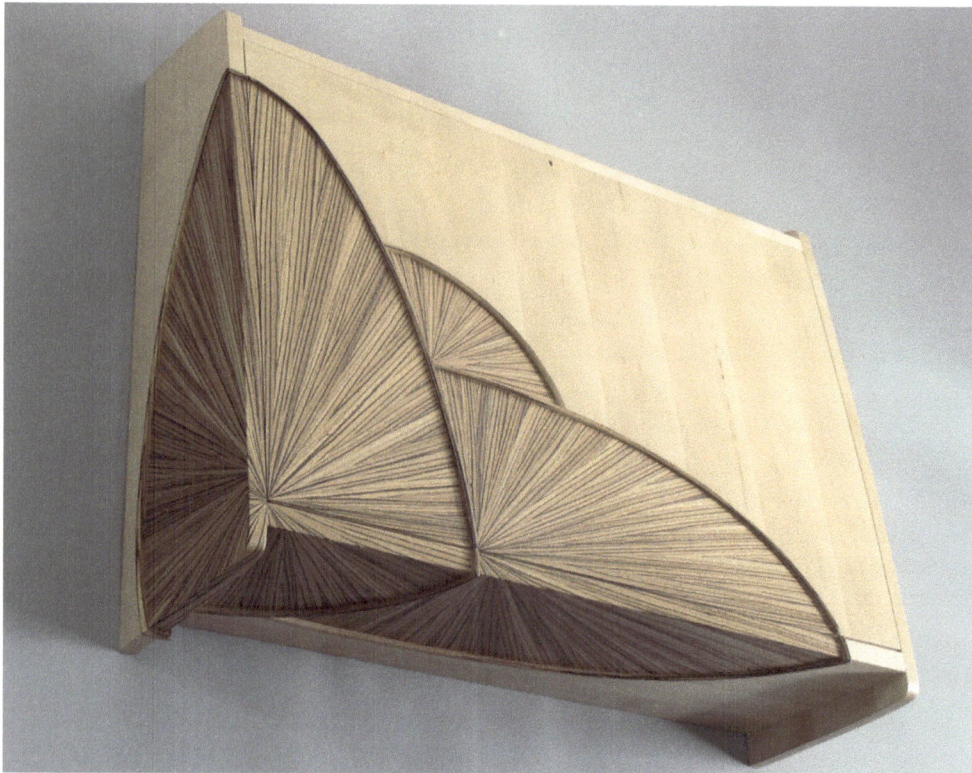

LIQUOR CABINET,
2013
EASTERN MAPLE,
ZEBRANO, CORK

24" H x 29.75" W
x 9" D

Jacques Breau
Ottawa, Ontario
Canada

**Photo by
Jacques Breau**

Photo by Ingeborg Suzanne Hardman

MODULAR CABINET, 2012 BLACK CHERRY, EAST INDIAN ROSEWOOD, SPALTED WESTERN
MAPLE, EASTERN MAPLE, NORWAY MAPLE 11" H x 23.5" W x 7.75" D
Jacques Breau Ottawa, Ontario Canada

LIQUOR CABINET,
2013
EASTERN MAPLE,
ZEBRANO, CORK

24" H x 29.75" W
x 9" D

Jacques Breau
Ottawa, Ontario
Canada

**Photo by
Jacques Breau**

DARK HORSE, 2014
WENGE, SPRUCE

24.5" H x 16" W
x 8" D

Jacques Breau
Ottawa, Ontario
Canada

**Photo by
Jacques Breau**

GALLERY
ALEXANDRA CLIMENT

AMOEBA TABLE,
2015
WAMARA CROSS-
SECTION,
METAL

22" D X 16" H

Alexandra Climent
New York, NY
USA

**Photo by
Julie Benedetto**

SPACE SHUTTLE TABLE, 2017 WAMARA STUMP, GLASS   42" D x 10" H
Alexandra Climent, New York, NY USA
Photo by Julie Benedetto

DECIENIAL TABLE 2017
SHIBADAN, GLASS,
SPALTED PENTAGLONE

32" D x 29" H

Alexandra Climent
New York, NY
USA

Photo by
Julie Benedetto

BOREALIS BOWL, 2016
WAMARA
HEARTWOOD,
SAPWOOD

4.5" D x 3.5" H

Alexandra Climent
New York, NY
USA

Photo by
Julie Benedetto

GALLERY
NORMAN PIROLLO

STANDING TALL, 2011
QUARTERSAWN CHERRY,
MAPLE, COCOBOLO

55" H x 15" W x 12" D

Norman Pirollo
Ottawa, Ontario
Canada

**Photo by
Linda Chenard**

WISHBONE TABLE, 2010
BLOODWOOD, MAPLE,
COCOBOLO, METAL
35" H x 43" W x 10" D
Norman Pirollo
Ottawa, Ontario
Canada

CHAOTIC CABINET,
2013
AMBROSIA MAPLE,
CHERRY, COCOBOLO

56.5" H x 18.5" W
x 13" D

Norman Pirollo
Ottawa, Ontario
Canada

**Photo by
Linda Chenard**

HALL TABLE,
2011
MAHOGANY,
METAL

36" H x 44" W
x 14" D

Norman Pirollo
Ottawa, Ontario
Canada

**Photo by
Linda Chenard**

GALLERY
PHILIP MORLEY

LOUNGE CHAIR,
2017
WALNUT,
SPALTED SYCAMORE

32" H x 26" W
x 30" D

Philip Morley
Wimberley, Texas
USA

**Photo by
Scott Cambridge**

Photo by Anna Mazurek

CHERRY BUFFET, 2017   CHERRY, WALNUT PULLS   35" H x 70" W x 21" D
Philip Morley   Wimberley, Texas   USA

LOUNGE CHAIR,
2017
WALNUT,
SPALTED
SYCAMORE

32" H x 26" W
 x 30" D

Philip Morley
Wimberley, Texas
USA

**Photo by
Scott Cambridge**

BLOOM TABLE, 2017
WALNUT, MAPLE

17" D x 28.5" H

Philip Morley
Wimberley, Texas
USA

**Photo by
Scott Cambridge**

DYNAMIC
DESIGN

Discussion of how to adapt an existing design to new criteria and data. The art of not finalizing a design until all possible variants have been investigated. How to keep an open mind about furniture design.

by Norman Pirollo

In recent years, I have added the new term dynamic design as part of my furniture design vocabulary. The term describes how a design can be modified to adapt to circumstances, for either technical considerations or for purely aesthetic reasons. Dynamic design is a term I coined to describe how design doesn't necessarily need to be cast in stone. It can instead be modified as a project progresses. The changes referred to can be either subtle changes or large scale changes. One of the meanings for the word dynamic from the American Heritage Dictionary.

dy·nam·ic – Characterized by continuous change, activity, or progress.

As my studio furniture is being created, the design originally envisioned can be improved at different stages. Alternatively, the original design can remain as is. Having this flexibility provides a continuous excitement for a studio furniture maker. It provides the advantage of enhancing the original design after seeing the furniture at various intermediary stages. An excellent example is a console table design I worked on a few years ago. I ultimately chose to invert the base of the table for aesthetic and technical reasons. This is not to say the original design of the maquette would not have worked. Inverting it solved a design dilemma and introduced a new aesthetic to the piece. After creating the maquette, I realized the need for a stable, strong sub-base to be able to support the V-shaped arch.

The console table base appeared small for the dimensions of the table top. Instead, inverting the base utilized the points of the arches as legs. Often, we become fixated on a particular design and do not seek out alternatives that often stare us right in the face. Case in point, I have been creating a new design for a smaller piece of furniture, and as part of my philosophy I strive to use as many materials in my possession as possible without continuously sourcing new material for the components. Working with material at hand sometimes limits what I can do, but on the other hand it challenges me to work within certain constraints. This is an instance of what I like to call dynamic design. Often the beauty of a design is in its simplicity. Simplicity is one of the tenets of the minimalism philosophy. I have to admit that I am an ardent fan of minimalism, and have read at least one book on the subject. You develop a different perspective on design after being exposed to the philosophy of minimalism.

I use maquettes as part of the design process. These reduced scale models of a furniture design help me better visualize the design in three dimensions. The maquette allows me to determine if both the proportions and aesthetic of a piece are fine as is or need improvement. It was while toying with the maquette for the hall table base that I discovered a different orientation for the base. Simply inverting the maquette provided a completely different perspective of the design. With this in mind, it became necessary to create a structure to firmly hold the table top, since the base is arched and the narrow top had minimal latitude to fasten a table top.

The new base design opened up the new possibility of creating a wishbone styled arch referred to earlier. The arched base could simply be an arch, but why not create an image of something else while maintaining the arch structure and shape? I looked at a few wishbone details and redesigned the arch to better reflect the shape of a wishbone. In the process, I also developed the semicircular support for the table top which was in harmony with the curves in the wishbone. The curved support would soon be a component of the curved table top.

USING DYNAMIC DESIGN CONCEPT TO EVOLVE A DESIGN
inverted base of scale model or maquette in the final design

This semicircular support actually evolved from the original maquette orientation as seen in the photo at left. It was also necessary to consider the harmony of the table. Do all the elements blend together well? I wanted a semicircular table top support to blend in with the table top. I created it using the same wood species as the top, in this case bloodwood. Bloodwood also nicely contrasted with the table base. Metal rods were used to attach the components. The cocobolo feet on each of the legs was a small touch included to draw some of the color down to the bottom of the wishbone shaped base and to create balance. Another criteria for the hall table was a narrow profile. This was included as a requirement in the design. The hall table was created with a narrow profile but maintained its stability. When this hall table was designed, I used predefined measurements for typical hall table designs. A curved top was incorporated into the design with its widest part at the peak of the wishbone arch. I hope to have enlightened you to the positive aspects of dynamic design through the use of maquettes as part of the design process.

DYNAMIC DESIGN

Designing a chair has its challenges. Unlike static pieces of furniture, the chair is moved around and is subject to stresses which test the type of joinery selected in its construction. In the lounge chair design shown on these pages, the design evolved from cardboard maquettes as seen below, to more advance prototypes seen on the following page. As can be seen, different configurations evolved from an original paper sketch. At one point, CAD renderings were introduced to provide a better 3-D perspective of the design. Unlike static pieces of furniture that remain in one place

and are not subject to shear type stresses, certain criteria need to be addressed in a successful chair design. The criteria includes comfort, strength, rigidity, weight, stability and of course the aesthetic of the chair. Dynamic design was applied to this design as seen in the different structural components. The design began with an open frame with triangle cutouts. The cutouts provide lightening while maintaining strength in the lounge chair design. Another version had lightening applied in the shape of differently sized lightening holes. The holes were created in groups of three in successively smaller sizes to follow the taper of each leg.

As the design evolved, other changes were implemented. The rake of the back, the width and length of the seat, were all modified as the design evolved. The changes were made to accommodate different sized people. Although there exist industry seating charts which specify optimal seat height, back size and height, and the rake of the back and chair, every chair is different. Since the most important criteria in a chair design is comfort, this single attribute had overwhelming priority in this design. As the design process evolved, the dynamic design principle was embraced in the design changes. Dynamic design allows a designer to factor new technical or aesthetic data into a design.

It is often only after a design has evolved into a full-scale prototype that a characteristic or element is noticed to be amiss. This could be the proportions of the design or it could involve the stability of the design as noted in the previously described console table design. Other design modifications that followed included the height of the seat back, the rake of the seat back and the depth of the seat itself. Although chair design conventions were followed, it was only after actual people sat in the full-scale prototypes that these measurements could be fine-tuned. In light of this, dynamic design was a large part of this chair design.

Chair design is probably at the extreme end of furniture design in that several unique criteria need to be considered. Every chair design is different. This lounge chair design had to have a particular rake to distinguish it from a dining chair. The rake of the seat and seat back were configured for a more relaxed seating experience. It is only after several prototypes were developed and created that the optimal seat size and angle were arrived at. In the design, the thickness of seat and seat back also factored into the seating experience. The seat thickness included thick foam padding with a leather covering. Together, the thickness of the seat and seat back reduced the available depth to sit on. It was necessary to include this important criteria in the final dimensions. Again, dynamic design was instrumental to the final outcome, since the thickness of the seat and back could only be factored in once the seat and back were part of the chair. The takeaway of this article is that design is hardly ever hard and fast. Often, it is only when a large scale mock-up of a furniture design is created that the eye notices a proportion is out of scale with other components of the design. The design itself can be found to be unstable where the depth or width of the piece is insufficient when measured against the height. Stability of a furniture piece becomes critical, especially in today's litigious environment.

Photo by Kyle Dorosz, 2017

ALEXANDRA CLIMENT
AN ORGANIC & SUSTAINABLE VIBE

by Norman Pirollo

A conversation with an up and coming sculptor and furniture maker from New York City. With a focus on sustainable and renewable resources, Alexandra shares the inspiration and methodology behind her intriguing, organic work.

In conversation with Alexandra Climent, her devotion to her craft is immediately obvious. The passion she displays in her work is second to none. Her creative journey began with trips to the jungles of South America and the ingenious idea of extracting the spoils of logging and then sculpting these into beautiful wood objects. It would be a disservice to leave behind the many stumps left from logging. Alexandria's vision was to have the world see the inherent beauty of figure and color in these remnants of logging. Working with local loggers, she overcame the challenge of pulling heavy and deeply rooted stumps and had them shipped to the US. Largely self-taught at woodworking, life unfolded and soon she was shaping and sculpting vessels, boxes, spoons and furniture pieces from this wood in her New York City studio. In her mission statement, Alexandra emphasizes the origins of the wood and that it is a sustainable resource.

For every stump removed, a new tree is planted. Alexandra judiciously carves and sculpts each of the objects by hand, a technique demanding copious amounts of patience and determination. Since the wood is naturally air-dried, it retains its exceptional color and figure. Alexandra describes how this tropical wood is among the hardest in the world and the difficulty of shaping and carving it. Nonetheless, she has developed a process to be able to perform this. Through Sustainably Sliced, she showcases her work and her successes in bringing awareness to this resource which would otherwise be lost. The passion demonstrated in her work is an inspiration to all creatives. The following questions were put to Alexandra to shed light on this up and coming sculptor and furniture maker. We look forward to seeing more of Alexandra's unique, exciting wood objects and furniture designs.

WS: As a champion of sustainably harvested forests, how and when did you decide to become a woodworker?

AC: I decided to become a woodworker after I fell in love with the beauty of exotic wood from deep in the jungle. During my travels to South America, I became fascinated with the idea of finding rare woods and making something from them. To me it was like digging up a rare gemstone in the middle of the jungle, which is such a complex place filled with so many challenges and obstacles. I had no background in woodworking, so I knew it was going to be a long journey. Little by little, mostly through trial and error, I taught myself how to make each piece.

WS: The woods you draw on for your work is sustainably harvested. Would you have it any other way? Does this positively impact your practice, knowing that this wood would have gone to waste instead.

AC: It is quite a strange feeling I have towards wood at this point. There have been times that I have picked up some scrap wood in the shop (a piece of walnut from another woodworker) and made a spoon to practice. After I made the spoon, I had no emotional attachment to it. It almost felt like cheating.... I didn't find this wood in the jungle, it was probably bought from some store... I actually hated the spoon and ended up hiding it and never looked at it again. So basically, I wouldn't and COULDN'T have it any other way. The biggest attachment I have to my pieces is not what I have made from them, but the material and where it came from.

WS: A little background of what draws you to raw wood in its natural state and how you shape it through carving.

AC: Usually when I am about to create a new piece, I have very little idea what I am going to make or which piece of wood I will use. Sometimes I will sit in the shop for over an hour just looking around at all the stumps and slabs I have in the shop. Most of the time I will start to see some characteristic of the wood that I don't want to change and I start thinking how I can work around it. For example, one of the last pieces I started working with was a stump. Around the bark was a weird indent that caused half the side of the stump to have a weird slope. When I peeled back the bark, a crazy pattern with spalting was revealed. I decided to use that part of the stump as the edge for a bowl and started to carve into the wood around it. It turned out to be one of my favorite creations.

WS: Growing up, is there a person or event that inspired you to follow a path in woodworking?

AC: The main event that influenced me to start woodworking was my interest in the jungle.. Before that, there was really nothing specific that pointed to woodworking. My father was always an extremely creative person and was both a guitar player and inventor. I always knew I wanted to be like him; creative. I wasn't cut out to have a 9-5 job. I always had to work since my family did not have a lot of money growing up and many of the jobs I had I hated with a passion. I knew I was meant for something else. I'm so grateful that I don't need to feel that way anymore now that I have found my passion.

WS: You appear to be self-taught. Have you studied woodworking or worked with a mentor?

AC: After years of working solely to get the wood from South America to NYC, when I finally got it here and was ready to actually work with it, I faced many challenges. I still had a full-time job and on my days off, my mom would come into the city from Long Island and she would drive me all over to try to find a wood shop or a mill to help cut my wood. All the places I went, they said they couldn't help. Most said the wood was too dense and could not be cut. Even mills with large bandsaws had no interest in helping me. It was so discouraging and I thought years of work may have gone to waste. I also didn't have enough money to get a studio of my own.

WS: You appear to be self-taught. Have you studied woodworking or worked with a mentor?

AC: One day I was walking around Brooklyn and heard a bunch of saws. Like a song you're drawn to, I followed the sound. It was a wood shop in Crown Heights and there were a bunch of people inside working. I shyly went inside and this guy introduced himself to me named Tony. I told him I was looking for space to work on some stumps and he said "well just come and share my space, i'm hardly ever here and I work mostly outside". The next day I was moving a few of my extremely heavy stumps in a tiny little space I was about to share with a complete stranger. I was also the only woman in the shop coming in with some very strange looking wood and I'm pretty sure everyone thought I was crazy. After many weeks of being in the shop, I had a bunch of woodworkers coming up and chatting about the wood and I let all of them all give their opinion on how I should be doing things. Some of the advice was great, but most of the techniques they employed did not work the same on the wood I had due to it's density. It was cool to see experienced woodworkers have to change their opinion and see how tough this stuff was to work with. So although I have gotten great advice from many of my woodworking friends, so much I have taught myself due to the nature of the material.

WS: You are a furniture designer, maker. What kinds of furniture do you design + build and in what styles?

AC: Pretty much everything I make is influenced by the grain of the wood. The colors that I uncover are so beautiful that they really shape what I will design. I like to keep the designs simple so that the wood can shine and speak for itself. I have designed a line of furniture and smaller items such as bowls, boxes and spoons. Each piece is one of a kind, but I am also able to do custom sizes in most pieces for clients, knowing that the wood grain will change and be different for every piece.

COLLECTION OF WOOD OBJECTS CREATING FROM SUSTAINABLY
HARVESTED WOOD, 2016
Alexandra Climent, New York, NY USA

Photo by Julie Benedetto

WS: You are also a skilled wood carver. How did you learn this and describe the experience of creating a hollow vessel from a wood blank.

AC: Carving into the wood I have is an extreme challenge due to the density of the wood. Most blades will burn out half way through using them, so I always work with machines and blades that are meant to cut metal. For larger pieces such as bowls, I will usually build a sled for a router and slowly burrow into the wood. This takes a very long time and usually by the time I am done, the bit for the router is completely burnt out. From there I will start shaping the inside by sanding with my hands. This process takes extreme patience. Most of the initial sanding is getting out the burn marks from the router. Most of my wood emits a resin when it burns that is very hard to sand. I make the spoons the same way, although I do not need to build a sled and use a much smaller router to make the initial hole in the cup of the spoon. From there I will use some very sharp carving tools and a ton of sanding to get the slope.

WS: How would you describe your current work and what inspires it?

AC: I would describe my work as if it were a ballet dancer. Strong, simple and seemingly effortlessly beautiful. The inspiration is always drawn from my travels back to the jungle and also from outer space. My father wrote a rock opera about outer space and he was quite obsessed with the idea of the universe. Many of my pieces are named after planets and alien groups in his rock opera.

WS: Do you have a favorite piece? If so, which one and why?

AC: I would say my favorite piece is the "Annular Platter". The reason I love this piece so much is partly because how difficult is was to make and how simple it appears. The "Annular Platter" was made from a cross-section of Pentaglone. The outside has the sapwood and as I burrowed into the heartwood, all the annular lines of the trees age was revealed. It's a very emotional piece for me to look at, seeing all the years the tree had grown and thinking about what was going on in the jungle at all those different times - what animals and organisms/fungi lived on the tree, the rain, the vines that grew etc.

WOOD VESSELS SCULPTED FROM SUSTAINABLY HARVESTED WOOD
Invictus Bowl, Irregular Borealis Bowl, Half Moon Cup, Borealis Bowl
Alexandra Climent, New York, NY USA   Photo by Julie Benedetto

WS: Which woods do prefer working with and why?

AC: Well, I prefer to only work with the wood I have found and obviously those are all extremely hard woods. I can't imagine working with any other types of woods at this point. Out of all the species I have, I would say that shibadan is one of my favorites because when you cut into it, it smells of tropical flowers.

WS: Are there any mediums that you haven't worked with yet but hope to in the future?

AC: I really would love to learn how to do more metalworking. Right now I rely on a few trusted people to make my bases when I have a client that wants a metal base, but I would much prefer to be able to do this myself.

WS: To date, what has been the most rewarding experience involving your furniture, carvings and being a woodworker?

AC: I would say the most rewarding moment so far was delivering the largest shelf I built and seeing it in it's new home. It was one of the toughest designs I had to do and it was such a large piece that it was very challenging to make the cuts and make sure it was built perfectly. After delivering that and seeing how beautiful it looked in it's new home, I felt like "wow, if I pulled that off, I can make anything happen".

Photo by Lily Olsen

COCLE CUSTOM SHELF, 2018
PENTAGLONE, BRASS
Alexandra Climent, New York, NY USA

DECIENIAL TABLE
2017
SHIBADAN, GLASS,
SPALTED
PENTAGLONE

32" D x 29" H

Alexandra Climent
New York, NY
USA

Photo by
Julie Benedetto

WS: What advice would you give to someone who is aspiring to become a woodworker and furniture designer?

AC: The first advice I would give would to be to find a little bit of time in your week and just start doing something. I get messages everyday from aspiring woodworkers and many times they don't know where to begin. I was certainly in this position before and all I can say is just jump in and don't be afraid or intimidated to make a mistake. Start with just sanding a piece and trying out finishing it. It may not be as cool as using a saw or a power tool, but it is one of the hardest things to master. Eventually you can start to use different machines little by little. Also, never be afraid to ask questions! Most other woodworkers are happy to give advice and guidance.

WS: What are you currently working on that you would like to mention?

AC: I just returned from a three week trip in the jungle where I have been endlessly searching for seeds of indigenous trees and gathering them to plant on my friend's farm. It has been very inspiring and I can't wait to see how that translates in the pieces I am going to be working on at the shop this week. I will be working on making some new bowls and a coffee table.

WS: Are there any upcoming projects and/or events that you would like to mention?

AC: I will be working on brand new art type pieces that will be displayed in Los Angeles at a few design shows and galleries. I will also be speaking at Maker's Central in the UK this May!

Sustainably Sliced

Presented by The Furniture Society

As our world becomes increasingly digital what is on the horizon for the world of furniture and objects? How will makers, artisans, artists, sellers, and consumers interact differently and create in new ways? And what key tensions will lead to the next big opportunities?

From June 13-16, 2018, the Furniture Society will explore these questions at the conference *NEXUS: Perspectives on Art, Design, Craftsmanship and Technology* in San Francisco. NEXUS will bring together the country's most visionary designers, artisans, technologists, futurists, and entrepreneurs to illuminate, provoke, and inspire. Join us!

Dogpatch Studios, 991 Tennessee St, San Francisco, CA 94107

More information on speakers and programming:
http://furnsoc.org/

Alexandra Climent
SUSTAINABLY SLICED
www.sustainablysliced.com
Instagram: @alexandracliment

POP
VENEERING YOUR FURNITURE DESIGN

by Norman Pirollo

Incorporate veneer into your furniture design and raise it to a new level of uniqueness. Veneer adds character to the aesthetic. Learn how to select, resaw, prepare and apply veneer to panels, both flat and curved.

Veneering enables the furniture created in your studio or workshop to be both more visually appealing and dimensionally stable. Veneered wood is simply a thin sheet of veneer glued to either solid wood or to a man-made material. A veneered panel is much stronger than solid wood. It will take considerably more effort to break a veneered panel than a solid piece of wood of similar thickness. A distrust of veneered work, common with people unfamiliar with wood, is likely due to poor construction techniques and the marketing of low quality veneered work as solid wood. Veneered work made a hundred years ago often comes apart in a modern heated home when the glue dries out. This occurs because glues used a century or more ago were not as reliable as glues today.

The structure of wood was also not well understood by craftsmen of that era. In addition, drawer fronts and table tops often warped because only a thin layer of veneer was applied to one side only. This causes a veneered panel to bow or cup with changes in humidity. Veneered pieces of solid wood are often badly warped or cracked, especially when the solid boards used as substrates are wide. Modern veneering processes prevent pieces from warping and cracking. Today, veneers are applied to both sides of a substrate to create stability. Solid wood furniture is more durable and resilient than veneered furniture.

Scratches, dings, dents, water marks, and stains can all be repaired on solid wood. It is simpler and less expensive to construct furniture using solid wood than with veneered panels. A disadvantage of solid wood is that exposure to extreme changes in humidity will cause the wood to expand or contract, and split along the grain of the wood. Advantages of veneer include having the best and most interesting logs sliced into veneers. This then becomes an economic decision. Distributors and veneer makers can make more money from a high quality log sliced into veneers than they can from sawing it into boards. Often, highly figured and exotic woods cannot be utilized unless they are sliced into veneers.

Slicing a figured or exotic board into veneers increases the yield acquired and the process becomes more sustainable. Slicing a board into veneers also eliminates the kerf introduced by a rotary saw blade. In large operations, the kerf is typically 1/4 inch. On a 1 inch thick board, this introduces considerable waste which ends up as sawdust. Commercial veneer is not cut but either rotary sliced with a knife or flat cut into 1/32 inch leaves or sheets. Veneering creates new design possibilities. Since veneer is so thin and glued to a stable substrate, designs and arrangements that would fail in solid wood can be achieved. Solid wood, even kiln-dried, will instead move through the seasons.

Selection of veneered panels using both commercial and resawn veneers

Cross grain designs in aprons and edge bandings are not possible with solid wood. Solid burls are typically unusable but can instead be used as veneers. Since veneer is glued to a dimensionally stable substrate, a surface not susceptible to warping, splitting or seasonal movement is created. Plywood and medium density fiberboard (MDF), the substrate or core materials typically used in veneering, are made from inferior quality trees. This creates a market for the landowner. This also leads to better forests, since the remaining trees grow better and quicker with less competition for resources.

One disadvantage is that veneer is easy to sand through when preparing for finishing. A piece which has been sanded through is almost impossible to repair and frequently involves a redesign of the piece, cutting off the sanded through area, or making a difficult repair which is difficult to hide. Once the furniture piece has been completed, veneer thickness is no longer an issue. To eliminate the veneer delaminating or lifting at edges, correct veneering methods need to be applied. Early in the 20th century, large quantities of low quality veneered furniture were made.

Construction techniques and materials have improved considerably in the past few decades to where delamination is no longer a concern. Hide glue is used in a few special applications and has been superseded by aliphatic (PVA) glues. Hammer veneering and complex, mechanical presses have been superseded by vacuum presses. Vacuum pressing ensures uniform clamping and expands design possibilities through the veneering of curved surfaces.

The aesthetic appeal of a veneered surface depends on the type of veneers used and how they are combined in figure and color to form unique and bold designs. The wilder and more irregular the grain figure of solid wood, the more the wood typically warps and checks while drying. Veneering is often the only way for such beautiful, highly figured woods to be used in a responsible manner.

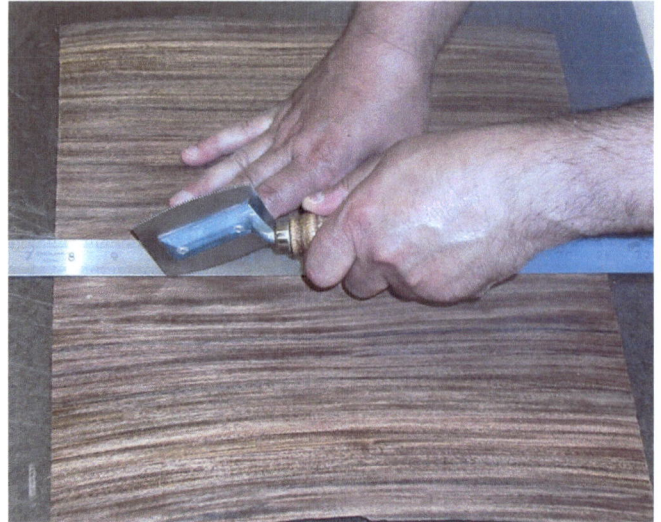

Top, slicing sheet of veneer
Middle, profile of flat veneered panel
Bottom, curved veneered panel

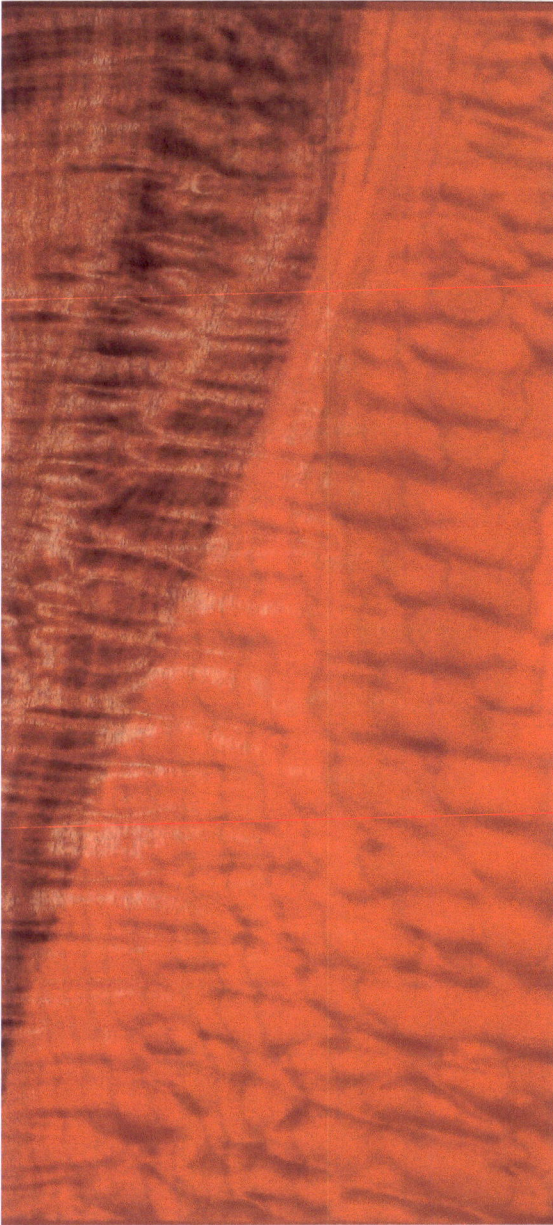

Veneers are typically sliced so thin, typically 1/28 in., that they must be glued to either straight grained or man-made cores to stay flat and perfect. Since veneer is glued to a substrate of a different wood or man-made material, for aesthetic reasons the edges must be covered. Edging a veneered panel involves applying a thin strip of solid wood that either matches the veneer or gives the appearance that the core or substrate is solid wood. In earlier times, hide glue was used since modern glues such as aliphatic or PVA glue, epoxies and urea formaldehyde did not exist. A feature of hide glue is that it is reversible, allowing joints and wood surfaces to be disassembled and reglued. Veneers applied with hide glues could therefore be removed and reapplied using a hot steam or dry iron when they lifted due to water damage. However, this process was not always successful.

Veneer sheets are joined in a factory where the joint is clamped together and stitched in a dedicated machine. Instead, glued paper tape or veneer tape is the only option for a woodworker or furniture maker. Veneer tape is widely used to splice or attach two pieces of veneer along a joint. Veneer tape comes in different weights and includes perforated holes. The holes allow the seam of the joint to be seen while gluing. It is critical that the seam have no gaps and the holes in the tape help to alleviate this. A heavier veneer tape is sometimes necessary for different species or types of veneer. This is mostly due to more flex and tension in the veneer. Veneers are dampened to flatten them prior to use. Veneer tape is easy to apply and to remove after gluing using a scraper.

Above, highly figured and dyed veneered board

Right, strips of veneer tape applied and taping veneer to substrate

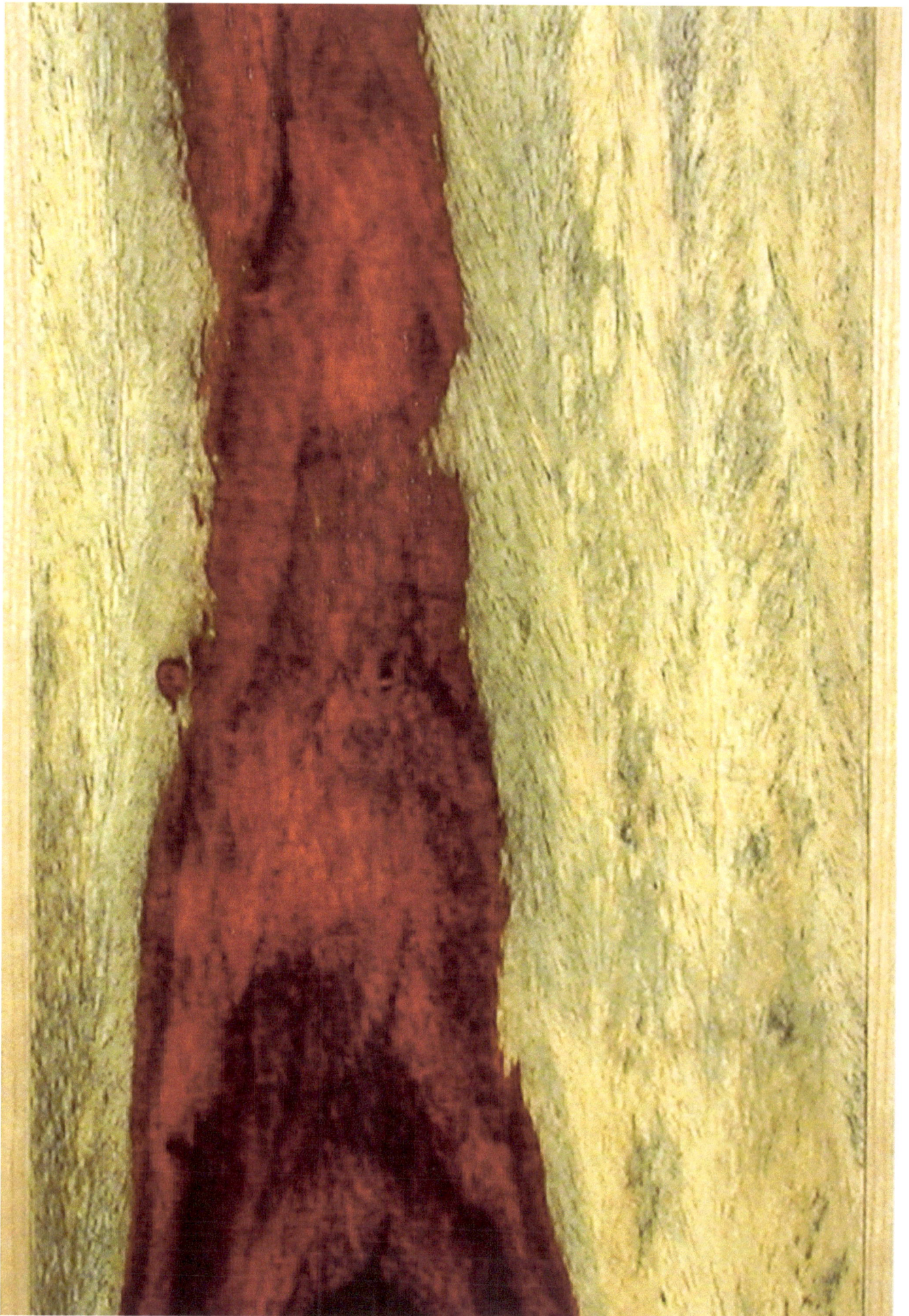

Knowledge of veneering is indispensable for a furniture maker, although solid wood furniture construction methods are very acceptable. Veneering has historically been important and it remains the unique method of achieving certain very attractive visual effects. Veneers vary from plain to highly figured or colored. This depends on the species of wood where certain woods can only be obtained in veneer form due to their scarcity. A second factor in determining figure is how the veneer was cut from the log, usually by rotary cutting or peeling, or by slicing in sheets.

Veneers can be obtained from a veneer supply house. They all sell bundles or flitches and some will also sell individual leaves of veneer, but not usually from the middle since that would break the sequence of a flitch. Small pieces of exotic veneers can also be obtained. Veneers can be glued down to both solid wood and to man-made boards such as plywood or MDF. These boards are known as substrates. On plywood, the veneer's grain should run at right angles to that of the face veneer of the board, the goal is to prevent any splits from appearing in the veneer as it moves with the substrate or plywood. On MDF, chipboard or man-made type material, this problem does not occur since the substrate is a very stable, monolithic material.

The advantages of veneering are numerous:

Quality face veneers cost far less than corresponding solid woods.

Many rare and beautiful woods are only available in veneer form and not in solid wood.

Properly veneered panels are stronger than solid wood and do not shrink, expand or crack with changes in humidity.

Being perfectly smooth, veneered panels are easier to finish and have a uniform appearance.

Veneering allows more dramatically figured woods to be used to enhance the beauty of a furniture piece.

Veneering is an environmentally preferred method of saving endangered tropical forests.

Another technique replacing conventional clamping and the mechanical veneer press is vacuum bag veneering. Vacuum bag presses are ideal since they exert an even force across the entire surface. Make sure to tape the veneer in place and cover with kraft paper or poly so it does not get stuck to the vacuum bag while gluing. Ensure that the panel is left in the clamps or press for the full drying time as dictated by the glue you are using. A discussion of vacuum bag pressing is slated for the next issue of this magazine.

Opposite page
Figured panel of padauk veneer with edging. Can be used as door panel of display cabinet.

Selection of commonly used veneering tools and veneer tape

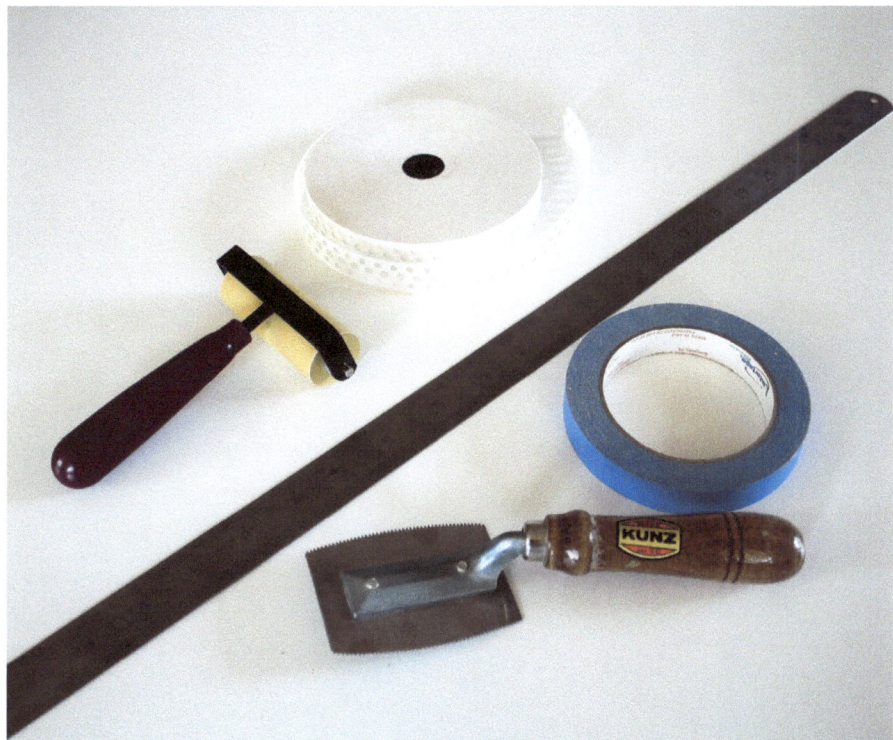

For clamping veneered work, handscrews and a couple of flat, thick boards can be used if the veneered piece is small. A more consistent clamping device, however, is a mechanical veneer press. Each unit or frame of a veneer press can be made with a span of 18 to 30 inches wide. A frame consist of an upper and a lower caul between two end posts and a press screw at each end of the upper bar. With two frames, stock up to 18 X 24 in. can be successfully veneered.

A veneer press can be made of wood as shown below. This mechanical veneer press is constructed using a series of cauls and threaded rods. The upper and lower pairs of cauls are slightly convex to deliver uniform clamping pressure along their length. The individual frames consist of upper and lower cauls attached close to the ends using threaded rods and wing nuts. The frames can be set into a jig as demonstrated below to keep them from moving or sliding while clamping is being performed.

The wing nuts at the threaded rods are individually torqued down until clamping pressure is uniform throughout. Platens are used above and below the veneered piece. These platens consist of 3/4 in. melamine coated man-made board or particleboard. One drawback is that this type of veneer press severely limits the size of veneer core you can use. You are essentially limited to the frame width and clamping jig length. The veneer press shown is typically used for smaller, flat veneered panels used in box-making. The threaded rods should be slightly lubricated with soap or graphite lubricant to keep from binding and to enable you to release the pressure after the veneered piece is dry. The cauls are usually made from a very hard wood such as maple or oak. The threaded rod size is typically 5/8 in. up to 3/4 in. for longer cauls.

When veneering a table top or other veneered surface, proceed as follows. If not using man-made boards, make the core or substrate of thoroughly seasoned, clear, straight grained wood because this warps the least. As a further insurance against warping, saw boards for the core or substrate into narrower widths at a maximum 2 to 3 inches. These are all glued together along their lengths to form the core or substrate of the veneered panel. When this glued up core is dry, plane one side perfectly flat either with a hand plane or thickness planer. Work carefully if hand planing, because if the core is not of the same thickness throughout, uniform pressure on all parts cannot be maintained in a veneer press. This may cause parts of the veneer to become unglued. After completing this step, the core or substrate is cut to size. When the core has been prepared, it can be crossbanded with inexpensive, straight grained veneer. These crossbanded veneers are glued at right angles to the solid wood core.

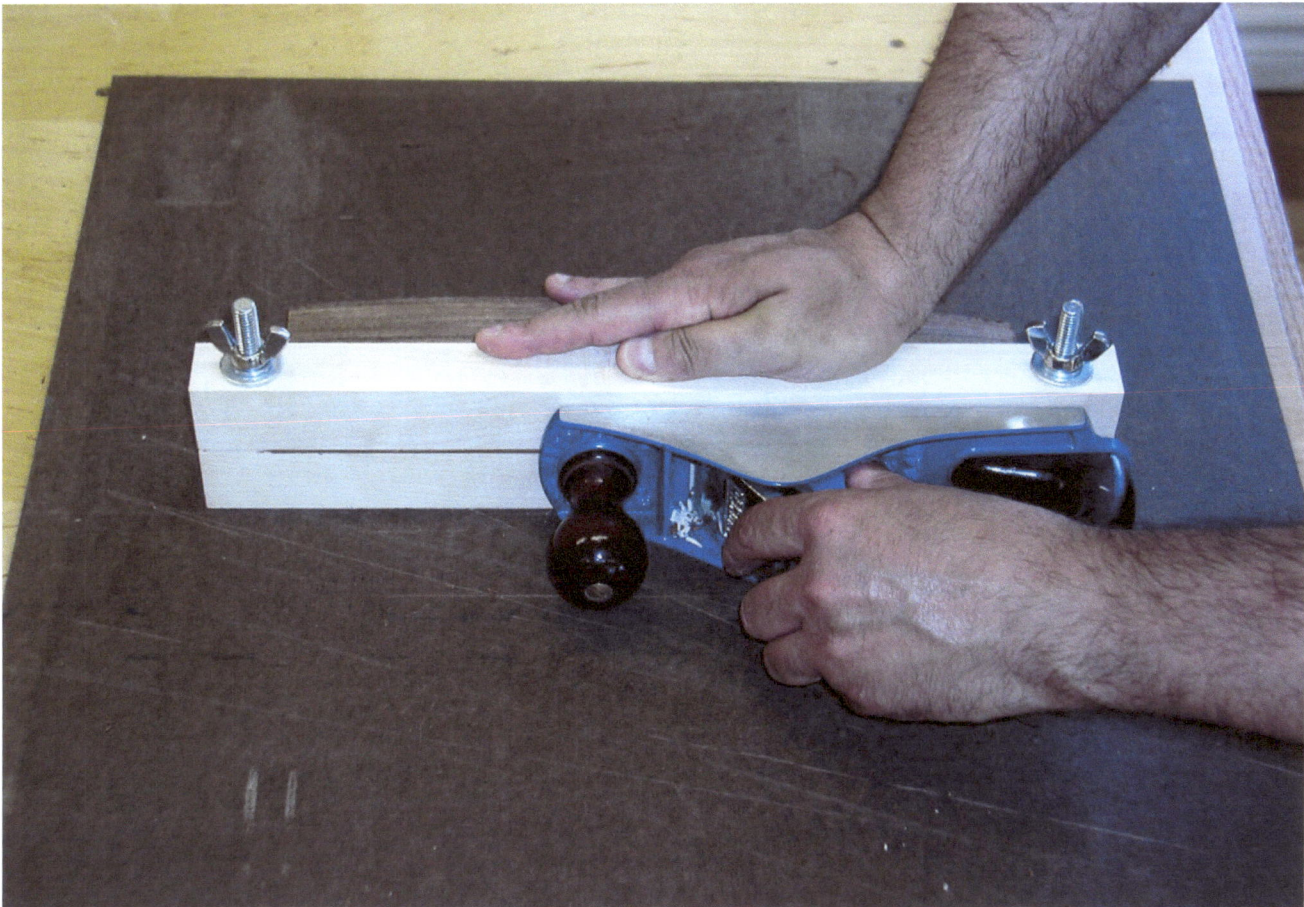

If the veneer used for crossbanding is not wide enough to cover surfaces at right angles, you can join their straight edges and tape them together. To plane or shoot edges straight, a clamping jig, shown above, must be made. This jig should have two cauls which are slightly convex in the center to provide adequate clamping in the center. The clamping jig for jointing veneers consists of 1 3/8 in. high X 1 1/8 in. wide pieces of hard maple or other hardwood. The cauls have a slightly convex form in the middle to maintain clamping pressure in the center of the jig. The clamping jig incorporates wing nuts for quick tightening. The carriage bolt heads are flush mounted.

The length can range from. 12 to 30 inches. 3/8 in. carriage bolts are used, and are 4 in. long each. Place the clamping jig on a bench and plane the veneer edges using a jack plane or longer plane. The veneers are then removed from the clamping jig and placed edge to edge on a board. If they fit together tightly, you can glue and tape them together using veneer tape. Veneer tape clamps the seam between the two pieces of veneer. The veneer tape is glued over the joint. Remember when gluing veneer with taped joints, the veneer tape should always be on top. The veneer tape is removed using a scraper after glue has dried.

Although commercial veneers are readily available, there are times when you prefer to saw your own veneer slices from a unique board with incredible figure. Commercial veneers are also very thin, less than 1/28 in. and can be very brittle and susceptible to buckling. Commercial veneers also tend to be somewhat expensive depending on the type of wood and quality of the veneer. If you set yourself up to be able to resaw lumber into thinner slices, you are well on your way to creating your own veneers. Resawing provides you the capability of slicing thick lumber into veneer pieces which can vary in thickness from as thin as 1/8 in. or greater. The preferred tool for resawing veneer is the bandsaw. On a standard 14 inch bandsaw, the depth of cut is typically 6 inches. This allows you to cut veneers up to 6 in. wide from thicker stock.

Several smaller 14 inch bandsaws have a riser kit available as an option. The riser extends the frame of the bandsaw up to 12 in. of throat height. This allows veneers up to 12 inches in width to be sliced. A more powerful motor is necessary to handle this extra capacity. A motor of a minimum 1 HP is recommended to be able to push through wide boards and clear the blade gullets of dust. The type of blade is also an important consideration. There are specially designed resaw blades for the bandsaw which make it easy to resaw lumber. Shown below is a 14 inch bandsaw set up for resawing. A riser block is installed and a 1 HP motor upgrade has been performed. The blades are now 105 in. long instead of the standard 92.5 inch length. This bandsaw also had the fence upgraded from the original fence. More efficient dust collection ports were added to the bandsaw as well as lighting. Resaw blade is a 3 TPI hook tooth style.

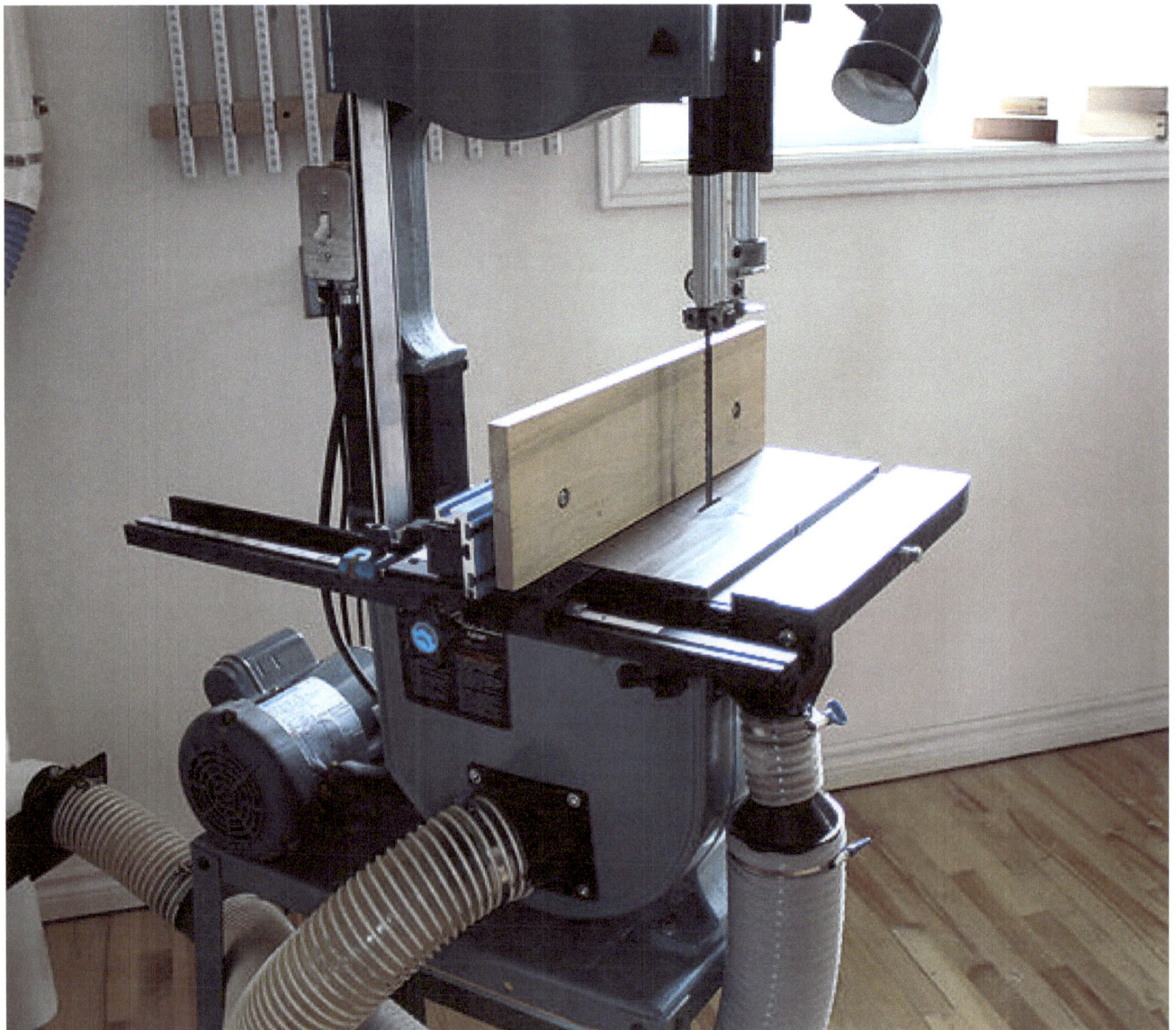

TAILS & PINS
THE CLASSIC JOINT

by Norman Pirollo

The dovetail joint has through the centuries denoted quality. Discover how to create accurate dovetails in both tail and pin boards. Elevate your designs by incorporating dovetail joinery. Through-dovetails discussed.

One of the most beautiful and striking woodworking joints is the dovetail joint. The dovetail joint is very often associated with quality woodworking. It is both a structurally strong and an aesthetically pleasing joint. Dovetail joints are often used in the construction of drawers, specifically drawer fronts. You also see dovetail joinery in case construction, where it creates a very strong, interlocking joint and enhances the quality. Several complex dovetail jigs are available that enable us to create dovetailed joints quickly and easily. However, most if not all of these dovetail jigs involve power tools. The hand cut dovetail, although more time consuming to create, offers unparalleled beauty in that any dovetail configuration can be realized. Dovetail joints are composed of pins and tails. In the photo below, the tails are being sawn while the tail board is clamped vertically in a vise. Once completed, the tail board is oriented horizontally in a dovetail clamping jig (shown later). The next step in the sequence will be to mark and transfer the tails to a pin board clamped vertically in the dovetail jig.

Creating dovetails by hand using a dovetail saw, chisels and marking tools, provide the flexibility to layout tail and pin spacing that is better suited to the drawer or case piece being constructed. The dovetail jig described in the next pages enables accurate marking and transferring of hand cut tails to a pin board. Once tails are transferred to a pin board, the dovetail jig is then used to chop out waste between individual pins. The top clamping cleat is used as a guide for the chisel. The dovetail jig is easily made and provides excellent accuracy and precision in creating hand cut dovetails.

Photo on previous page shows dovetail joints created using only hand tools. The contrast between a light tail board and a darker pin board is striking. In drawer construction, the thicker piece is a drawer front whereas the thinner piece is the drawer side. The spacing and width of individual pins and tails are customized to suit the piece. On previous page, the dovetail joint at left is an example of through dovetail joinery, whereas the right image is a half-blind dovetail joint, where the tails are enclosed in the pin board. Both through and half-blind joinery are used in drawer construction.

Above, a process called the divider technique is used to lay out the tails for a dovetail joint. Although there are alternative approaches to laying out the tails, the divider technique shown involves no arithmetic. The width of the divider is adjusted to where three tails can be marked in the approximately 3 in. space between the outside half-pin lines. One point of the divider is placed exactly on the half-pin line. With little pressure applied, the divider is rotated across the end of the board three times. It is important to adjust the divider to the number of tails desired. In this case three tails were decided on and a little trial and error provides a good spacing of the divider points. Upon the third rotation as seen above, a point of the divider reaches past the outside half-pin line. This distance from where the divider point passes the line becomes the distance between the tails. As seen, this space is approximately 3/16 in. A trial and error process can be used to arrive at a spacing you prefer. In this case, three 15/16 in. tails with 3/16 in. spacing between them were decided on. There are therefore four 3/16 in. tail spacings required including the half-pin divisions. The 3/16 in. distance between the middle tails was decided using previous experience in cutting tails.

It is necessary to leave enough wood between the tails to be able to successfully create two saw kerfs between them. The spacing arrived at has wide tails and narrow pins. This distinguishes handmade dovetails from machine made dovetails where spacing between tails and pins is often uniform. In the photos on the next page at top and bottom, typical dovetail tools and a dovetail jig are shown. The dovetail jig is used for both chopping out pin sockets and to then transfer tails to the pin board. Although other methods of chopping out the tails exist, it is found that using this dovetail jig greatly reduces the incidence of chopping out too far back. The top cleat prevents this situation. The set of dovetail tools shown is typical, but a few of the tools can be substituted. For example, a sliding bevel gauge can be substituted for the small square dovetail marker. The saw, although very specific for cutting dovetails, can be substituted with a narrow kerf, fine toothed saw. This selection of hand tools is used in the creation of hand cut dovetails. Typical tools include layout and marking tools, chisels, a dovetail saw and mallet. Laying out and marking is of utmost importance in the creation of precision dovetail joints.

Dovetail tool selection above, chopping out tails below

At bottom left, a series of relief cuts were performed with the chisel oriented vertically to the board. A narrower chisel, as seen, is then used to lift a piece of wood from each of the pin sockets. The thin triangular wedges of pin socket waste are popped off. It is important to not disturb any of the wood comprising the actual tails while performing this chopping technique. After continuing to chop and remove wood from the pin sockets, the two-step procedure of lifting and removing a triangular piece of waste wood from the pin sockets continues. A 1/8 in. chisel is used to lift the triangular wood waste from the pin sockets. This procedure is continued until the bottom of the pin socket is reached.

As seen above, the tails have now been prepared. It is then a matter of transferring the tails to the pin board and then chopping out the tail sockets. In the photo on the next page, the careful transfer of the tails to the pin board determines how tight and gap free the dovetail joint will be. A thin, sharp knife is used to transfer the tails to the pin board. Once the tails have been transferred to the pin board, the process of sawing the pins begins at bottom of the next page. Important considerations are to keep the saw blade horizontal to avoid sawing past the baseline. As well, check the tracking of the saw on either face to ensure it is tracking correctly. One side of the marked lines is sawn for the pins much like the process followed for sawing the tails. There are six cuts to perform with three cuts sawn on one face and the board then flipped around to create the other three saw cuts.

The saw cuts are then continued from the flip side of the pin board. Saw kerfs can be seen on one side of the marked lines. The acquired skill of sawing to the pencil or knife line is critical in this procedure. A knife marking is typically very thin whereas a pencil line is fat in comparison. The knife mark is filled in with a pencil line for clarity. The likelihood of gaps between the tails and pins can be eliminated by sawing to the correct side of the pencil line. With practice, sawing to the pencil line can be perfected. A piece of advice in developing this technique is to practice sawing to either side of a pencil line on a scrap board. Practicing of sawing prior to sawing the actual dovetails or pins will reduce or eliminate any incidence of error. Practice sawing can be performed on a scrap board as well.

Transferring and marking the tails to the pin board above, sawing the pins below

Next, the pin board is clamped horizontally in the dovetail jig and the baseline of the pins is aligned with the bottom front edge of the upper cleat. This procedure is very similar to that of chopping waste from the tails. A wide chisel is then selected to begin the chopping operation. Creating relief cuts and chopping out each of the tail sockets is next. The process followed is to tap the chisel down and to then to remove material from the tail socket. As shown below, the removal of waste wood from the tail sockets follows. This technique can be difficult to perform free hand or without using a dovetail jig. It is critical that the tail socket be square to the face to ensure the pins fit both correctly and tight against the tail board. Alignment of the pin baseline is ensured through use of the clamping cleat where the chisel enters the waste section perfectly vertical to the face of the pin board. The dovetail jig shown excels in this method. Once the pin waste has been chopped out, the pins are tuned to match the tails created earlier.

Above, final chopping of the waste is being performed prior to flipping the board over and continuing to clear the remaining waste. The board is flipped over to create clean chisel cuts on either face of the board. The pins have now been almost completely chiseled out. Afterward, paring of the corners of each tail socket opening is performed. The extra wood on the sides of the openings is pared with a wide, sharp chisel. A word of caution. To avoid injury, never place a hand directly in front of a chisel while paring! Next, any remaining waste is pared to the marked lines. The pin board is clamped to the dovetail jig, serving as an ideal base for this operation.

Care is also taken not to gouge the surface of the jig. For this reason, a very thin sheet of hardboard is placed between the surface of the dovetail jig and the pin board. On the following page, the completed pins can be seen from either face of the pin board. Afterward, the pins continue to be cleaned out and tuned to ensure the mating tails fit perfectly. This is often a trial and error procedure where the tail board is temporarily fit onto the pin board and any binding is checked for and addressed. The completed tight-fitting dovetail joint can be seen on the next page.

Cleaning and tuning the pins above, completed dovetail joint below

ébénisterie endgrain woodworks

IG: @endgrainwoodworks
jbreau@endgrain.ca

jacques breau
endgrain.ca

WoodSkills
Instructional woodworking courseware

newart
P R E S S

Photo by Austin Waldo

PHILIP MORLEY
FROM PROCESS TO DETAIL

by Norman Pirollo

A candid conversation with Philip Morley reveals his background and the inspiration for his exceptional one of a kind furniture pieces. Discover more about his journey from England to the US, both literally and figuratively.

In conversation with Philip Morley, one is immediately struck by his folksy, down to earth character. From humble beginnings in England, Philip now calls the USA home. A graduate of the intensive and structured English Guild system, he describes how the focus of an English Guild education is very traditional with an emphasis on hand tool use. After relocating to the USA, he apprenticed for several years with Michael Colca, to whom he holds in absolute highest regard as a master craftsman. Philip goes on to say that Michael Colca was instrumental in shaping his professional furniture making career. Philip has since set up his own furniture making shop outside Austin, Texas. Today, Philip creates beautiful one of a kind furniture with the occasional small batch run of his more popular designs. From chairs to freestanding cabinets and tables, he welcomes design challenges.

Philip enjoys combining art into the functional aspect of furniture design. As a follower of James Krenov's philosophy and inspiration, he conveys how much of an influence James Krenov has been on his practice and how he has embraced Scandinavian design as a consequence. Philip describes how he combines machines, jigs and hand tools in his work. Machines to expedite the initial phase of a build, jigs and hand tools to shape and sculpt the components. He also has no qualms in sharing his knowledge with up and coming woodworkers. Philip currently teaches woodworking part-time at ACC in Austin, Texas. The following questions were put to Philip to shed more light on this rising craftsman and furniture maker. We look forward to seeing more of Philip's unique and exciting furniture designs in the future.

Philip Morley Furniture

WS: Growing up in England, who and what inspired you to follow a path in woodworking?

PM: In a way, woodworking chose me. I suffered academically in school being diagnosed later on with dyslexia. I went to a school for troubled teens. It was there that I met a woodshop teacher who really took me under his wing. It was a new experience for me. I found something I was actually good at and enjoyed. Once I finished high school, I had to decide whether to go to trade school and which trade to do. It only made sense to continue into a carpentry and joinery program.

WS: Your woodworking background is in the English Guild system, tell us what this was like? How does it compare to woodworking instruction in North America?

PM: In my experience, being a part time teacher at ACC (perhaps the closest thing to a trade school here) it is vastly different. The English Guild program was pretty intensive. It was five days a week and 8 hours a day. They training you to come out as a professional and be able to get a job. There was a very clear and established program. You could take year 1-3. If you completed the whole program you would get a card verifying your completion of the program which enabled you to get a job. There were also job opportunities lined up for the students. The third year, students split their time between college and job experience. So, you left feeling very prepared for a specific line of work. Each semester you progressed to a higher level of complexity in joinery. We learned about traditional roof construction, stair making, window and door making with a huge emphasis on safety and quality.

WS: How much emphasis is placed on hand tool use in the English Guild system?

PM: There was a huge emphasis on hand tools. The first year, we were only allowed to use hand tools with the notion that you learned how to do it by hand tools, it gave you a better understanding of the process and how wood behaves before we were allowed to use power tools. Even when we were allowed to use power tools, there was a huge emphasis on hand tools. But instead of having to mill a piece of wood S4S we were allowed to use power tools. But a lot of the joinery was still done by hand. A lot of the students that came out of the program were going to work on restoration projects. One of the most common skills required was how to swing a door properly. . . . chopping your own butt hinges in and how to install a mortise-lock or any other hardware. For the first year of me working on site, you were not allowed to use any power tools (router, etc) until you proved that you were capable.

WS: As a furniture designer, maker, what kinds of furniture do you design, make and in what styles?

PM: I build free standing furniture. I don't do kitchens or built ins. Most of my work is chairs, dining tables, beds, case work (buffets, etc). I typically work with a client that usually comes to me because they like my aesthetic in design and I will make a one-of-a-kind piece for them while still making it my own. I am heavily influenced by Scandinavian design (James Krenov. . . as mentioned:):)) Also countless others. But I really like clean-line work. . . not necessarily modern. I love a piece that packs a lot of details that may go unseen until you live with it for a little while.

WS: How would you describe your current work and what inspires it?

PM: I love designing and I love challenging myself on every piece that I do. I try to push the design limits and technical aspects of the piece without making it look overly complicated. I like a piece to be complicated but not look complicated. I get a lot of inspiration off Instagram and seeing what other furniture makers are doing.

ROCKING CHAIR, 2017 WALNUT, BRASS (Detail) Philip Morley Wimberley, Texas USA

WS: Do you have a favorite piece? If so, which one and why?

PM: I think my favorite piece is my lounge chair. I love the look and the detail but I also love that it is the true meaning of functional art. It is comfortable and beautiful to me. It makes me happy to see it when I walk into a room. It gets used, touched, it is functional. . . . I am sitting in right now. :) I like that it has a mid-century modern vibe but it also has an artisan aspect with the sculptural joinery and the small details throughout the piece (the profiling of the edges and arms, the exposed bridle joints, etc)

WS: You combine both power tools and hand tools in your work. At what point of a build do you break out your hand tools?

PM: Obviously it depends on the job but every job that leaves my shop will have some hand tool work.. . . . not necessarily out of nostalgia but hand tools can simply do things that power tools cannot. A lot of times it is in preparing the wood for spraying. I use a lot of hand planes and some of my chairs there are sculptural parts to that I have thought about making a jig to do but I enjoy the process and honestly just don't feel like you could get the same look and feel that you can accomplish with the hand tools.

Photo by Anna Mazurek

CHERRY BUFFET, 2017 CHERRY, WALNUT (Detail) Philip Morley Wimberley, Texas USA

WS: You enjoy working with small multiples of a design. At what point do you move on to another design and do you revisit earlier designs?

PM: Really I have two or three pieces that I continue to build. These are typically chairs. As soon as I sell out of a particular chair and things calm down or I get a specific order. If someone orders a rocking chair, I schedule it in and make 5-7 at a time. Sometimes I make small changes even on those designs as I grow and am around the design more. There is always somethings that can be improved. How I think of my shop really is somewhat of a prototype shop. Most of the things that leave my shop are one-off pieces that I have designed for a particular client to suit their needs.

WS: How much of an improvement in your processes have woodworking jigs made. Has the precision and repeatability improved?

PM: There probably isn't a job that I do (even on one-off pieces) that I don't do some kind of jig for. Even on one piece there are particular elements that must be repeated throughout the piece and repeatability and accuracy and safety are extremely important. So, yes, I find jigs to be incredibly important. Of course with my chairs, I cannot imagine building them without a batch of jigs. Although, I am always amazed by how long it takes.

WS: Which woods do prefer working with and why?

PM: Walnut- I love how rich the wood is. I love the purples and reds and variation of color within the walnut. It is incredibly nice to work with.... easy on hand tools and milling. With most woods, if I could have my absolute way, every stick of wood I got would be rift-sawn. I guess I am kind of boring but I love straight tight grain in wood. Cherry is a very classic wood and really has all the same properties and workability as walnut. I love how cherry ages over time. I am also liking rift-sawn white oak. I actually may have some lounge chairs coming up in white oak. I am not as crazy about the workability but I love its strength, density and texture. It is just a good solid wood.

Photo by Scott Cambridge

LOUNGE CHAIR, 2017 WALNUT, SYCAMORE (Detail) Philip Morley Wimberley, Texas USA
This photo and photo on facing page

WS: Are there any mediums that you haven't worked with yet but hope to in the future?

PM: Yes. Absolutely. I would love to learn how to weld and I would also love to take some machinist classes. I always wanted to get into jewelry making as far as casting and making my own hardware.

WS: To date, what was most rewarding experience involving your furniture and as a woodworker?

PM: Honestly, I would have to say when Fine Woodworking asked me to write an article as a contributing author. I grew up with this magazine (not even being able to read it but taking in as much as I could from the pictures) and I got a lot of inspiration from it. So, I think it meant a lot to me to be included in this publication.

WS: What advice would you give someone aspiring to be a woodworker and furniture designer?

PM: I would say get out and do it. I think it takes experience and time to learn this skill. I think books can only get you so far you have got to practice, take risks, and be ready to make mistakes. I am a big believer in apprenticeships. I apprenticed for 7 years under a master craftsmen and I give my mentor, Michael Colca, absolute credit for accelerating my professional career. I think I learned more from him in those years than I ever could have done on my own. Other advice would be, don't quit your day job until you get your feet on the ground. Work out of your garage until you figure out where you want to go and what you want to do. As far as design, I would say find someone that inspires you. Don't necessarily copy but explore what it is you like about that design. Keep thinking about ideas and possibilities. Sketch a lot. Don't let technical aspects prevent you from trying a cool design. Get started on it and you can figure out the technical aspect as you go.

WS: What are you currently working on that you would like to mention?

PM: I am currently working on a really awesome executive desk made out of walnut with brass inlay. It will include a whiskey bar and hidden drawers.

WS: Are there any upcoming projects and/or events that you would like to mention?

PM: I think the project I am most excited about is a love seat version of my lounge chair and also a new bed design. Those are the things that I am most looking forward to.

Photo by Scott Cambridge

FURNITURE DESIGN
ORIGINS & PROCESS

by Norman Pirollo

In this article I describe an earlier furniture design of mine and the methodology followed in arriving at the final design. The design is a jewelry armoire where the actual dimensions were finalized after close consultation with my client and discussion of their needs. The client was seeking a particular style and after producing a few sketches and drawings we arrived at a design compromise. The woods used, the design, proportions, and detail work were all discussed over initial meetings.

Several structural factors were considered in the design since the final height of the armoire was sixty-five inches high and did not occupy a very deep or wide footprint. The tall height introduced the issue of stability. This was overcome by maintaining a minimum depth and width for maximum stability in light of the small footprint of the armoire. The client also granted me artistic freedom to embellish the design and to include elements which would add to the uniqueness of the piece. Since the style for the cabinet or armoire was contemporary, there was no preexisting furniture period to draw ideas from.

For obvious reasons, the jewelry armoire was designed to have its contents completely hidden. This criteria of the design was a given in the preliminary design. I worked with the Golden rectangle and carcase ratios as much as possible yet it was necessary to modify the proportions for both functional and aesthetic reasons. The functional reasons were essentially the stability of the armoire given its height, width, and depth. The aesthetic of the form was developed specifically to keep the the armoire proportion to the minimum depth necessary. The joinery used in the armoire involved mortise and tenon construction for the door members and ganged dowel joinery for the main carcase.

The rear of the armoire consisted of a frame and panel back completely rabbeted into the frame of the armoire. Interior joinery consisted of dovetailed drawers. The cabinet base will be discussed a little later once the topic of furniture design is broached. The armoire and base were designed as two separate sections for ease of transport. It made more sense to build this way. It was also decided to incorporate tapered legs with contrasting toe caps for the legs. This was uncharted territory for me at the time. To add to this, an element of string inlay was added to the individual legs.

Dovetailed drawer fronts with contrasting drawer pulls. Inlay elements also visible

Some discussion follows of how furniture design has evolved over the centuries. If we go back to the middle ages and the era before, quite a few developments in furniture construction techniques occurred. Prior to this era, in earlier centuries, very little furniture was available for the masses. It was considered a luxury to have chairs, tables and cabinets. Larger, more finely made furniture of this era was typically destined for the aristocracy of the time, as a display of their wealth and status. Interestingly, most conventional furniture of these early periods was assembled without consideration for wood expansion and contraction or wood movement. This was not an issue for many years, since the interior of buildings during this period of history was often at the same temperature as the exterior. With the advent of heated interiors, wood movement became much more of a factor to deal with in construction and design of furniture. The practice of simply assembling wood planks together to form furniture needed to evolve. It was in the middle ages that frame and panel construction was adopted. This technique allowed a solid wood panel to literally float within a wood frame composed of rails and stiles. The solid wood panel could expand and contract on a seasonal basis, and not cause any structural failure within the furniture.

All of a sudden, more possibilities were created for furniture design and its widespread appeal began in earnest. Furniture also began to become more affordable as of the 18th and 19th century. More furniture makers existed and sound construction techniques began to be standardized. There are numerous periods over the past centuries and each of these had a style or styles associated with them. Additionally, each country had developed a style of its own during these periods. It can be seen how similar furniture design principles were adopted by successive countries over the different periods. Popular furniture styles that are widely recognized have familiar names such as English Chippendale, German Biedermeier, American Federal, Arts & Crafts, French Art Nouveau, Italian Rococo, etc. The evolution continues to more recent styles such as Modern Swedish (Krenov style) and Contemporary styles. One interesting note is that a style of furniture is never really defined until the particular period has elapsed, almost like looking through a rear view mirror. Today's styles might be referred to as a certain style period, but only after the period has lapsed.

Frame and panel construction revolutionized furniture design

Curved elements combined with straight elements and an alternative medium

I occasionally ask myself, what constitutes good design. Is it the aesthetic of the piece, the pleasing proportions, the balance of form and function, or all these characteristics combined? Taking a step back, the aesthetic and pleasing proportions are definitely at the forefront. I am usually drawn to a piece of furniture that stands out with respect to the appearance of the piece. This unique characteristic causes me to stop and further examine the piece where I attempt to understand what has drawn me to this particular design over another design. This analysis helps me in my design process to better understand what characteristics of a piece of furniture I am drawn to. Of course, we all have different styles of furniture that we are drawn to, but the overarching common theme is good design. I am convinced that even an admirer of period styles of furniture will stop at a well-designed modern piece of furniture to further analyze it. We've all heard the saying that everything has already been discovered or invented. I have even heard this saying applied to furniture design. After all, we're reshaping the same objects over and over.

Curves are added, proportions changed, ornamentation is added and ornamentation removed, darker or lighter woods are used, curved elements introduced, thick and thin components used. Furniture design is in essence derivative. One style of furniture utilizes elements from an earlier style. Occasionally, a completely new radical furniture design is created with little to no resemblance to an earlier design period. It is easy to come to the conclusion that everything has already been done. However, I regularly see new pieces of furniture that make me sit back and say: "wow, that is an interesting or cool design, I wonder if it's been done before". In light of this, I think the boundaries of design are limitless, one just needs to think outside the box. Also, I feel that using preexisting styles as templates for a new design sometimes handicaps the designer. The designer subconsciously has the existing style in mind and cannot get past it. Often, it is better to begin with a clean slate. Start with a pad and pencil and begin to sketch without any existing furniture designs to influence your new design.

I occasionally spend time researching past furniture styles. It is often mentioned that much design today has already been done, and after seeing some good examples of period furniture, there is some truth in this old adage. My favorite influential maker is George Hepplewhite and the furniture associated with his era. Furniture of the late 18th century has been mostly characterized by Chippendale and the cabriole leg design element. George Hepplewhite, however, is much less written about and known. His furniture style was characterized by the slight, tapered legs of his furniture and the lightness and delicacy in his pieces. A considerable amount of 20th century furniture has been derived from this late 18th and early 19th century period. In particular, furniture derived from the makers Chippendale and Hepplewhite. American Federal style furniture had its origins in the Hepplewhite style. Much of the design elements of this particular period have made their way into furniture of the past century.

This can be considered a revival of a previous style in time, but I like to think of it as simply embracing design elements which were and continue to be pleasing to the eye. When I flip through examples of furniture representative of previous periods and styles, it is easy to see what worked and what didn't work. The design elements which are pleasing and well-proportioned are carried into later periods, whereas the not so pleasing elements typically die off. Another trend noticed is how previous styles of furniture are sometimes renounced and discarded only to be replaced with a radically different style of furniture. We see this very same phenomenon today in everything ranging from fashion, automobiles, and continue to see it in furniture styles. A revival of a previous period or style of furniture then occurs, much like what occurs in the fashion world today.

Inclusion of both rectilinear and curved design elements
MODULAR CABINET, 2012 11" H x 23.5" W x 7.75" D
Jacques Breau Ottawa, Ontario Canada

Photo by Ingeborg Suzanne Hardman

Decorative inlay elements, fan inlay and shell inlay used to enhance furniture

The reason for describing this design trend can be valuable to furniture makers today. As makers, we all have our favorite styles. It may be important to incorporate proven design elements in our designs, elements that have demonstrated the most success over the centuries. Since the furniture we are designing is often derived from a previous style or work, it makes more sense to derive elements from successful styles of furniture. Although I am a huge fan of clean, simple lines with minimal adornment, I like to incorporate some inlay into my work. The inlay sparks my creativity and in a strange way provides me the impetus to complete the furniture piece to get to the part of adding inlay detail. A piece of furniture can be compared to a large canvas where the inlay is the artwork. Other makers might define themselves through another feature in their work, perhaps some carving or marquetry. George Hepplewhite often distinguished his work with added inlay.

A large proportion of Hepplewhite and Federal style furniture is inlaid with the exotic woods which had come into popularity by the late part of the 18th century and early 19th century. This concludes the brief discussion on furniture design. Continuing on with the earlier discussion of the design of the legs, they were completed following a detailed process. The legs and aprons were completed after allowing the raw components to release internal stresses and tension which might have developed. These internal tensions were released in the resawing performed for both the leg blanks and aprons. I began with a wide plank of 8/4 cherry for the legs and ripped four leg blanks from this blank. Each leg blank was oriented on the plank to attain the best possible grain configuration. In this case, a rift-pattern with no face grain on any of the leg faces was sought after. This process is more wasteful of wood, but it is worth the effort. The leg blanks selected had a pleasing straight-grained orientation on all four faces.

Afterward, I marked and created the mortises for the mortise and tenon joints at each leg. Since the armoire or cabinet had already been built, it was necessary to create the stand with the exact dimensions in length and width to appear integral. This was a greater challenge than anticipated, since the measurements were very critical and needed to be exact. The cabinet and stand needed to appear as one unit. Therefore, it was necessary to measure the aprons with allowance for the legs at either end and for the tenons. The tenons had four shoulders completely housed within the joint as well as being offset on the face of the legs towards the front. There was a bit of trial and error involved. A small trial joint with similar dimensions was created to test for measurements, since the apron faces would need to be flush with the leg surfaces. After some deliberation, it was decided the safest approach would be to create the mortises first, then cut the aprons slightly longer than final length and then cut the tenons. I now had the final measurement of the front, back and sides.

I worked back from this by subtracting the thickness of the already prepared leg blanks. This process worked well and I was able to slowly sneak up on the final measurement for the apron. A shoulder plane is a godsend in this situation, as it is specifically designed to trim and tune tenon shoulders. Continuing with this process, I often checked that the tenon and shoulder were square and perpendicular to the apron. Shortly afterward, the four aprons were ready. The stand was since been assembled using clamps and the cabinet test fit on it. Next step was to taper the legs. The design on these tapered legs has a taper beginning a few inches below the apron to the foot of the leg. Only the two inner faces of the legs are tapered. The tapers were rough cut using a bandsaw and afterward it was strictly hand plane work using a jointer plane. It is very rewarding to watch the tapers being created without too much effort and without use of fancy jigs, only with hand planes. The stand components were then completed. The next step was to create the decorative detail work on the front apron.

Shaping legs for cabinet base

Tie-in of door pull elements with inlay detail of front apron

I proceeded to add decorative detail work on the front apron of the stand for the armoire. Since this cabinet was essentially a jewelry armoire, a diamond theme for the inlay detail was decided upon. The pattern created on the apron for the stand provides the appearance of holding the armoire up. The center diamond in holly balances out the theme and provides a contrast to the outside blackwood half-diamond and stringing elements. As with most anything woodworking related, the inlay work involved precise measurements since the pattern is symmetric. Working on and creating the inlay detail was immensely enjoyable although a little stressful at times since the spare apron I had set aside somehow developed a ding. The stand by now was completely assembled and has been test-fitted with the armoire attached. Wood pins or dowels were used to connect the armoire and stand together. This feature made it simple to separate the two pieces for transport and for any other reason to separate them. Next was to work on the decorative door pulls. I decided to embed some holly into the blackwood pulls to carry the blackwood and white holly colors from the stand to the armoire.

There is also a subtle inclusion of holly in the door pulls with a continuation of the diamond theme. The door pulls have a small tenon with four shoulders which fits into a chiseled recess in each of the doors. The door pull recesses were carefully marked until it was confirmed that the pulls were perfectly aligned in both planes. At the center of the front apron is a holly diamond. Holly and blackwood were selected to provide good contrast once the cherry ages and develops a darker color and patina. There is no stain applied to my work. Instead, I let the natural aging process of cherry develop its own distinct color. Woods with natural contrasting colors are used as often as possible. More work remained on the armoire, mostly completion work. It was necessary to install two brass carousels and a few brass pegs, create compartments in the drawers, and to line the drawers. The focus now shifted to getting the detail correct. The surfaces were lightly scraped to prepare for finishing. This is the point where the emphasis shifts to applying finish and work could also begin on the drawer compartment and individual drawers and drawer dividers.

A short while later, the front door pulls were created and installed. It was now beginning to look like a complete cabinet on stand. The door pulls were designed with a half-diamond embedded at the front, this carried the diamond theme into the armoire cabinet. This effect introduced the right balance of color in the armoire as well as creating a subdued but striking appearance. I did not want to remove focus from the tiger maple door panels but instead establish a fine symmetry in the colors of the cabinet. A hint of white holly in the door pulls made the difference in creating harmony. The armoire was now oriented and secured to the stand with only a single pin on either side. The pin is essentially a short length of dowel. The cabinet or armoire could now be easily detached from the stand. This feature allowed me to continue with the next phase of work. There was specialized hardware to install in the interior of the cabinet, but this could wait until two or more layers of shellac finish were applied. The first phase of the finishing process involved lightly scraping all surfaces, removing pencil marks, and checking for markings I would not want under the finish.

The finish was thinned shellac applied in multiple coats with an applicator pad. This was a lengthy process as each coat is thin. Only after several coats does the finish begin to attain the right sheen and depth. A few years ago I had begun using more natural finishes on my furniture pieces. The benefits to this were primarily health motivated. As well, natural finishes are pleasant to use and with the right consistency can be applied with an applicator pad. My finish of choice has been thinned clear or super blonde shellac with a light coat of wax afterward. I mix my own shellac from fresh shellac flakes and perform the finishing over a period of a few days. Shellac coats dry quickly so the possibility of dust nibs on the surface are next to nil. Many thinned coats guarantee a nice, even finish if the strokes of the applicator pad are offset to overlap every so often. Within a few days it was fascinating to see how much the upper cabinet had naturally darkened compared to the stand which was only recently assembled. This disparity in color would blend together over the next two weeks, one of the great features of cherry.

Pirollo Design

More detail of drawers and drawer pulls

PHILIP MORLEY
Custom **M** *Furniture*
WIMBERLEY, TEXAS

Philip Morley
Custom Furniture
Wimberley, Texas
www.philipmorleyfurniture.com
Instagram: @philipmorleyfurniture

---

pirollo
design

Norman Pirollo
Custom Furniture
Ottawa, Ontario Canada
www.pirollodesign.com
Instagram: @pirollodesign

CLOSING THOUGHTS

by Editorial Team

This will be the end of the first issue of WOODSKILLS magazine. We sincerely hope the new format and contents of the magazine have provided insight to the furniture maker's featured in this issue and provide you reason to return for the

It is the objective of the editorial team at WOODSKILLS to have provided you an enjoyable experience with this issue. Having been exposed to countless magazines over decades, we collectively discovered a niche for a different genre of woodworking magazine. A magazine with a focus on the reasons behind a furniture design. Instead of detailed furniture construction steps, WOODSKILLS delves into the thought process behind a furniture design. As well, we describe how specific techniques and processes will advance you as a woodworker and furniture maker. The emphasis of this magazine is hand tool use, where machines can be used in the initial phase of a furniture build to prepare blanks from rough sawn timbers. Well-researched time and labor-saving precision hand tool techniques are put forward and discussed in every issue. We are not averse to the use of machines where it makes the most sense. It is wiser to emphasize hand tool use in the latter stages of a furniture build where meticulous attention to detail is necessary and preferred.

An analogy is that of a long distance runner who maintains a steady pace early on and later sprints to the finish. Homage is paid to classic techniques such as dovetail joinery, mortise and tenon joinery, and time-proven hand tool methods. It is our belief that traditional furniture construction methods and processes should be maintained and passed on to future generations. As testament to their reliability and longevity, traditional methods have evolved little over the centuries. As well as the traditional, we put forward modern techniques and processes that make your furniture designs stand out and be unique. Our focus is one of a kind furniture, the unique furniture and wood objects that separate their makers from every other maker. Each issue includes profiles and candid conversations with established furniture designers and makers. Find out what they are passionate about, what drives them and where they draw inspiration from. Often, reading about a furniture maker instills in us the enthusiasm and impetus to break through and move forward. It is not so much how but the why behind the process that is often critical in a furniture maker's mind and practice.

Inside Back Cover
ROCKING CHAIR, 2017
WALNUT, BRASS ACCENTS
49" H x 23" W x 42" D
Philip Morley Wimberley, Texas USA

Outside Back Cover
SHOWCASE #1, 2007
SPALTED WESTERN MAPLE,
PORT ORFORD CEDAR,
BROWN DOUSSIE,GLASS
48" H x 26" W x 13" D
Jacques Breau Ottawa, Ontario Canada